THE USBORN
PICTURE
DICTIONARY
IN FRENCH

Angela Wilkes
Illustrated by Colin King
Translated by Katherine Folliot

Consultant: Betty Root

| Fifi | Mimi | Sam Strongman | The dogs | Pop |

Aa

to add **ajouter**

Aggie ajoute du sucre au thé.
Aggie adds sugar to the tea.

afternoon **l'après-midi (m)**

Viens me voir cet après-midi.
Come and see me this afternoon.

Il fait du football l'après-midi.
He plays football in the afternoon.

about **sur**

Voici un livre sur les dragons.
This is a book about dragons.

address **l'adresse (f)**

Voici l'adresse d'Henri.
This is Henry's address.

again **encore**

Henri a eu encore un accident.
Henry has had an accident again.

above **au-dessus de**

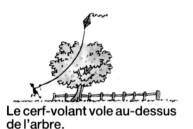

Le cerf-volant vole au-dessus de l'arbre.
The kite is above the tree.

aeroplane **l'avion (m)**

Cet avion est vert.
This aeroplane is green.

against **contre**

Fifi s'appuie contre un mur.
Fifi leans against a wall.

accident **l'accident (m)**

Henri a un accident.
Henry has an accident.

to be afraid **avoir peur**

Le chien a peur des souris.
The dog is afraid of mice.

age **l'âge (m)**

Ces hommes ont le même âge.
These men are the same age.

actor **l'acteur (m)[1]**

Voici un acteur célèbre.
This is a famous actor.

after **après**

Mardi vient après lundi.
Tuesday comes after Monday.

Il est arrivé après minuit.
He arrived after midnight.

Le chien court après le chat.
The dog runs after the cat.

air **l'air (m)**

L'avion est en l'air.
The aeroplane is in the air.

1. actress: **l'actrice (f)**

| airport | l'aéroport (m) | along | le long de | ambulance | l'ambulance (f) |

Le pilote voit l'aéroport.
The pilot sees the airport.

Des fleurs poussent le long du chemin.
Flowers grow along the path.

L'ambulance arrive.
The ambulance is arriving.

---

alarm clock — **le réveil**

Le réveil sonne.
The alarm-clock is ringing.

alphabet — **l'alphabet (m)**

Chaque lettre est dans l'alphabet.
Every letter is in the alphabet.

among — **parmi**

Le chat est parmi les oiseaux.
The cat is among the birds.

---

all — **tous, toutes**

Toutes les souris sont roses.
All the mice are pink.

already — **déjà**

Mimi a déjà un gâteau.
Mimi already has a cake.

and — **et**

Voici Fritz et Hank.
Here are Fritz and Hank.

---

almost — **presque**

Il a presque fini.
He has almost finished.

also — **aussi**

Mimi est une fille; c'est aussi un bébé.
Mimi is a girl; she is also a baby.

Fifi n'est pas seulement belle, elle est aussi intelligente.
Fifi is not only beautiful, she is also clever.

angel — **l'ange (m)**

L'ange vole.
The angel is flying.

---

alone — **seul**

Fifi est toute seule.
Fifi is all alone.

always — **toujours**

Henri a toujours des accidents.
Henry always has accidents.

angry — **en colère**

L'ange est en colère.
The angel is angry.

| animal | l'animal (m) | apple | la pomme | army | l'armée (f) |

Ce sont tous des animaux. *
These are all animals.

Fifi mange une pomme.
Fifi is eating an apple.

Bill est dans l'armée.
Bill is in the army.

| another | un/une autre | apron | le tablier | to arrange | arranger |

Bill prend un autre gâteau.
Bill takes another cake.

Bill met son tablier.
Bill puts on his apron.

Fifi arrange les fleurs dans un vase.
Fifi arranges the flowers.

| answer | la solution[1] | to argue | se disputer | to arrive | arriver |

Voici une addition et sa solution.
Here is a sum and its answer.

Bill et Ben se disputent.
Bill and Ben argue.

Le train arrive.
The train arrives.

| ant | la fourmi | arm | le bras | arrow | la flèche |

La fourmi court sur le livre.
The ant runs over the book.

Ben a le bras cassé.
Ben has a broken arm.

Holmes trouve une flèche.
Holmes finds an arrow.

| any | des | armchair | le fauteuil | artist | l'artiste |

Avez-vous des oeufs?
Have you any eggs?

| anybody | quelqu'un |

Y a-t-il quelqu'un ici?
Is anybody there?

Le chat est sur le fauteuil.
The cat is on the armchair.

L'artiste peint.
The artist is painting.

1. **La solution** only means the answer to a sum. The word for an answer to a question is **la réponse**.

as	**lorsque**

Il pleuvait lorsque nous sommes partis.
It was raining as we left.

	comme

Comme il pleut, il reste chez lui.
As it is raining, he is staying at home.

to ask (for)	**demander**

Mimi demande une pomme.
Mimi asks for an apple.

astronaut	**l'astronaute (m)**

Voici un astronaute.
Here is an astronaut.

at	**à, au**

À quatre heures nous prenons le thé.
At four o'clock we have tea.

Les enfants sont à l'école et Ben est au travail.
The children are at school and Ben is at work.

aunt	**la tante**

Tante Aggie est la soeur de maman.
Aunt Aggie is Mum's sister.

baby	**le bébé**

Le bébé pleure.
The baby is crying.

back	**le dos**

Henri se gratte le dos.
Henry scratches his back.

bad	**mauvais**

Il fait mauvais aujourd'hui.
The weather is bad today.

Papa est de mauvaise humeur.
Father is in a bad mood.

Elle a un mauvais rhume.
She has a bad cold.

badge	**le badge**

Bill porte beaucoup de badges. *
Bill is wearing many badges.

---

bag	**le sac**

Le sac est plein d'argent.
The bag is full of money.

baker	**le boulanger**

Le boulanger fait le pain.
The baker makes bread.

ball	**le ballon**

Max attrape le ballon.
Max catches the ball.

balloon	**le ballon**

Mimi joue avec un ballon.
Mimi plays with a balloon.

banana	**la banane**

Un gros régime de bananes.
A big bunch of bananas.

---

2. **Le ballon** is the word used for a big ball. A small ball is **la balle.**

band **la fanfare**	bath **la baignoire**	bear **l'ours (m)**

La fanfare joue.
The band is playing.

Le chat est dans la baignoire.
The cat is in the bath.

Bruno est un ours brun.
Bruno is a brown bear.

bank **le bord**

Jim est au bord de la rivière.
Jim is on the river bank.

bathroom **la salle de bains**

La baignoire est dans la salle de bains.
The bath is in the bathroom.

beard **la barbe**

Cet homme a une longue barbe.
This man has a long beard.

bank **la banque**

Fred quitte la banque en courant.
Fred runs away from the bank.

beach **la plage**

Fifi est allongée sur la plage.
Fifi is lying on the beach.

beautiful **beau, belle**

Une belle princesse.
A beautiful princess.

to bark **aboyer**

Le chien aboie.
The dog is barking.

beak **le bec**

L'oiseau a un bec rouge.
The bird has a red beak.

because **parce que**

Le bébé pleure parce qu'il a faim.
The baby is crying because it is hungry.

Il est gros parce qu'il mange trop.
He is fat because he eats too much.

basket **le panier**

Le panier est plein de pommes.
The basket is full of apples.

bean **le haricot**

Voici des haricots* verts.
These are green beans.

bed **le lit**

Le roi est au lit.
The king is in bed.

| bedroom | la chambre | to begin | commencer | below | au dessous de |

Le lit est dans la chambre.
The bed is in the bedroom.

Il commence à pleuvoir.
It is beginning to rain.

Le match commence.
The match is beginning.

Le film commence à sept heures.
The film begins at seven o'clock.

Le chat est au-dessous de Bruno.
The cat is below Bruno.

| bee | l'abeille (f) | behind | derrière | belt | la ceinture |

L'abeille est sur une fleur.
The bee is on a flower.

Qui est derrière l'arbre?
Who is behind the tree?

Fifi a une grosse ceinture.
Fifi has a big belt.

| beef | le boeuf | to believe | croire | bench | le banc |

Bob coupe le rôti de boeuf.
Bob is carving the beef.

Sam croit à mon histoire.
Sam believes my story.

Sam croit tout ce qu'on lui dit.
Sam believes anything you tell him.

Papy croit en Dieu.
Pop believes in God.

L'oiseau est sur le banc.
The bird is on the bench.

| beer | la bière | bell | la cloche | to bend | plier |

La cloche sonne.
The bell is ringing.

Sam fait plier une cuiller.
Sam is bending a spoon.

Bill boit de la bière.
Bill is drinking beer.

| before | avant | to belong to | appartenir à | best | le meilleur / la meilleure |

Lundi vient avant mardi.
Monday comes before Tuesday.

Il est arrivé avant minuit.
He arrived before midnight.

Bill se lève avant Ben.
Bill gets up before Ben.

Le chapeau appartient à Ben.
The hat belongs to Ben.

À qui ceci appartient-il?
Who does this belong to?

Ceci appartient à Fifi.
It belongs to Fifi.

Fifi est la meilleure danseuse.
Fifi is the best dancer.

He is the best in the class.
Il est le meilleur de la classe.

better	mieux

Fifi danse mieux que Susie.
Fifi dances better than Susie.

Henri parle français mieux que Ben.
Henry speaks French better than Ben.

birthday	l'anniversaire (m)

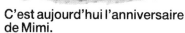

C'est aujourd'hui l'anniversaire de Mimi.
Today is Mimi's birthday.

blanket	la couverture

Une couverture rouge sur le lit.
A red blanket on the bed.

between	entre

Le chat est entre deux ours.
The cat is between two bears.

to bite	mordre

Le chien mord le facteur.
The dog bites the postman.

blind	aveugle

Un chien guide l'aveugle.
A dog leads the blind man.

bicycle	la bicyclette

Le boulanger est sur sa bicyclette.
The baker is on his bicycle.

black	noir

Le gros chat est noir.
The big cat is black.

blood	le sang

Sam a du sang sur le doigt.
Sam has blood on his finger.

big	gros, grosse

L'éléphant est gros.
The elephant is big.

blackbird	le merle

Un merle est noir.
A blackbird is black.

to blow	souffler

Mimi souffle les bougies.
Mimi blows out the candles.

bird	l'oiseau (m)

L'oiseau est perché sur une bicyclette.
The bird is on a bicycle.

blackboard	le tableau noir

Ben dessine au tableau noir.
Ben draws on the blackboard.

blue	bleu

La maison est bleue.
The house is blue.

boat	**le bateau**

Trois hommes dans un bateau.
Three men in a boat.

body	**le corps**

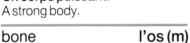

Un corps puissant.
A strong body.

bone	**l'os (m)**

Fluff a un grand os.
Fluff has a big bone.

bonfire	**le feu de joie**

Le feu de joie brûle bien.
The bonfire is burning.

book	**le livre**

Voici un livre sur les bateaux.
This book is about boats.

---

bookshop	**la librairie**

Bill va à la librairie.
Bill goes to the bookshop.

boot	**la botte**

Cet oiseau a une botte bleue.
This bird has a blue boot.

both	**les deux**

Les deux cochons sont roses.
Both the pigs are pink.

bottle	**la bouteille**

Une grosse bouteille de vin.
A big bottle of wine.

bottom	**le bas**

La grenouille est en bas de l'échelle.
The frog is at the bottom of the ladder.

---

bowl	**la coupe**

Une coupe pleine de bananes.
A bowl full of bananas.

box	**la boîte**

Le chat dort dans une boîte.
The cat sleeps in a box.

boy	**le garçon**

Tom est un petit garçon.
Tom is a little boy.

bracelet	**le bracelet**

Mimi porte un bracelet bleu.
Mimi is wearing a blue bracelet.

branch	**la branche**

L'oiseau est sur la branche.
The bird is on the branch.

11

bread	le pain	bride	la mariée	brother	le frère

Bill coupe le pain.
Bill cuts the bread.

Une belle mariée.
A beautiful bride.

Bill et Ben sont frères. *
Bill and Ben are brothers.

to **break**	**casser**	**bridegroom**	**le marié**	**brown**	**brun**

Ben casse le pain.
Ben breaks the bread.

Et le marié.
And her bridegroom.

Bruno est un ours brun.
Bruno is a brown bear.

breakfast	**le petit déjeuner**	**bridge**	**le pont**	to **brush**	**brosser**

Fifi prend son petit déjeuner.
Fifi has her breakfast.

Bill traverse le pont.
Bill crosses the bridge.

Fritz brosse ses chaussures.
Fritz brushes his shoes.

to **breathe**	**respirer**	**bright**	**brillant**	**bubble**	**la bulle**

Les poissons respirent sous l'eau.
Fish breathe underwater.

Une étoile brillante.
A bright star.

L'ours fait une bulle.
The bear blows a bubble.

brick	**la brique**	to **bring**	**apporter**	**bucket**	**le seau**

L'homme porte une brique.
The man is carrying a brick.

Max apporte une pantoufle à Bill.
Max brings Bill a slipper.

Bill vide le seau.
Bill empties the bucket.

12

bud	**le bourgeon**

La plante a un bourgeon.
The plant has one bud.

to build	**construire**

L'homme construit une maison.
The man is building a house.

building	**le bâtiment**

Une maison est un bâtiment.
A house is a building.

bulb	**le bulbe**

Une chenille regarde le bulbe.
A caterpillar looks at the bulb.

bull	**le taureau**

Le taureau poursuit Bill.
The bull chases Bill.

bulldozer	**le bulldozer**

Ben conduit un bulldozer.
Ben drives a bulldozer.

bump	**la bosse**

Henri heurte une bosse.
Henry hits a bump.

bunch	**le bouquet**

Un gros bouquet de fleurs.
A big bunch of flowers.

burglar	**le cambrioleur**

Le cambrioleur se sauve.
The burglar runs away.

to burn	**brûler**

La maison brûle.
The house is burning.

bus	**l'autobus (m)**

L'autobus s'arrête.
The bus is stopping.

bus stop	**l'arrêt d'autobus (m)**

Fifi attend à l'arrêt d'autobus.
Fifi waits at the bus stop.

bush	**le buisson**

Qui est derrière le buisson?
Who is behind the bush?

busy	**occupé**

Cet homme est très occupé.
This man is very busy.

but	**mais**

Bill mange beaucoup mais il n'est pas gros.
Bill eats a lot but he is not fat.

J'aime les bonbons mais pas le chocolat.
I like sweets but I do not like chocolate.

butcher **le boucher**	by **à côté de**	cake **le gâteau**

Le boucher vend de la viande.
The butcher sells meat.

L'homme est à côté de la voiture.
The man is by the car.

Fifi coupe le gâteau.
Fifi cuts the cake.

butter **le beurre**		calculator **la calculatrice**

Le beurre fond.
The butter is melting.

L'homme se sert de sa calculatrice.
The man uses his calculator.

butterfly **le papillon**	cabbage **le chou**	calendar **le calendrier**

Un papillon sur une fleur.
A butterfly on a flower.

Fifi choisit un chou.
Fifi chooses a cabbage.

Aggie regarde le calendrier.
Aggie looks at the calendar.

button **le bouton**	café **le café**	calf **le veau**

Fifi coud un bouton.
Fifi sews on a button.

Les amis vont au café.
The friends go to a cafe.

Un veau avec sa mère.
A calf with its mother.

to buy **acheter**	cage **la cage**	to call **appeler**

Fifi achète des bananes.
Fifi buys some bananas.

Le lion est dans une cage.
The lion is in a cage.

Le fermier appelle le veau.
The farmer calls the calf.

14

| camel | le chameau | capital | la capitale | carpet | le tapis |

Rome est la capitale de l'Italie.
Rome is the capital of Italy.

Paris est la capitale de la France.
Paris is the capital of France.

Henri monte sur un chameau.
Henry is riding a camel.

Le tapis est bleu.
The carpet is blue.

| camera | l'appareil-photo | car | la voiture | carrot | la carotte |

Bill a un nouvel appareil-photo.
Bill has a new camera.

Fred conduit une voiture rapide.
Fred drives a fast car.

Une botte de carottes. *
A bunch of carrots.

| to camp | camper | caravan | la caravane | to carry | porter[1] |

Bill et Ben campent.
Bill and Ben are camping.

Il a aussi une grosse caravane.
He also has a large caravan.

Mimi porte des carottes. *
Mimi is carrying carrots.

| candle | la bougie | card | la carte | castle | le château |

Henri porte une bougie.
Henry is carrying a candle.

Un jeu de cartes. *
A game of cards.

Le château est sur une colline.
The castle is on a hill.

| cap | la casquette | cardigan | le cardigan | cat | le chat |

Fred porte une casquette.
Fred is wearing a cap.

Aggie porte un cardigan rose.
Aggie is wearing a pink cardigan.

Le chat est sur le tapis.
The cat is on the carpet.

1. porter also means "to wear".

to catch	**attraper**

Le chat attrape le ballon.
The cat is catching the ball.

caterpillar	**la chenille**

La chenille mange une feuille.
The caterpillar is eating a leaf.

cauliflower	**le chou-fleur**

Un chou-fleur dans un panier.
A cauliflower in a basket.

cave	**la caverne**

Il y a un trésor dans la caverne.
There is treasure in the cave.

ceiling	**le plafond**

Sam touche le plafond.
Sam touches the ceiling.

cellar	**la cave**

Le vin est dans la cave.
The wine is in the cellar.

chain	**la chaîne**

La montre est attachée à une chaîne.
The watch is on a chain.

chair	**la chaise**

Bruno est assis sur une chaise.
Bruno is sitting on a chair.

chalk	**la craie**

Bruno écrit avec de la craie.
Bruno is writing with chalk.

change	**la monnaie**

Bill compte sa monnaie.
Bill counts his change.

to change	**changer**

Henri change une roue.
Henry changes a wheel.

to chase	**poursuivre**

Henri poursuit un voleur.
Henry chases a thief.

cheap	**bon marché**

Ce fauteuil est bon marché.
This armchair is cheap.

cheek	**la joue**

Mamie a les joues roses.
Nan has pink cheeks.

cheese	**le fromage**

Fifi mange du fromage.
Fifi is eating cheese.

chemist	**le pharmacien**	chicken	**le poulet**	chips	**les frites (f)** *

Henri est chez le pharmacien.
Henry is at the chemist's.

Ben découpe le poulet.
Ben is cutting the chicken.

Sam a une assiette de frites.
Sam has a plate of chips.

cheque	**le chèque**	child	**l'enfant (m)**	chocolate	**le chocolat**

Bill fait un chèque.
Bill writes a cheque.

Les enfants jouent.
The children are playing.

Mimi mange du chocolat.
Mimi is eating chocolate.

cherry	**la cerise**	chimney	**la cheminée**	to choose	**choisir**

Un oiseau mange les cerises. *
A bird is eating the cherries.

L'oiseau est sur la cheminée.
The bird is on the chimney.

Fifi choisit une robe rouge.
Fifi chooses a red dress.

chest	**la poitrine**	chimpanzee	**le chimpanzé**	chop	**la côtelette**

Sam se frappe la poitrine.
Sam is beating his chest.

Un chimpanzé dans un arbre.
A chimpanzee in a tree.

Ben mange une côtelette.
Ben is eating a chop.

chick	**le poussin**	chin	**le menton**	Christmas	**Noël**

La poule a cinq poussins.
The hen has five chicks.

Sam se frotte le menton.
Sam rubs his chin.

C'est Noël.
It is Christmas.

| church   l'église (f) | city   la ville | clever   intelligent |

Fifi va à l'église.
Fifi goes to church.

New York est une grande ville.
New York is a big city.

Un homme intelligent apprend vite.
A clever man learns fast.

| cigarette   la cigarette | class   la classe | cliff   la falaise |

Cet homme fume une cigarette.
This man is smoking a cigarette.

Il y a cinq enfants* dans la classe.
There are five children in the class.

Henri est sur une falaise.
Henry is on a cliff.

| cinema   le cinéma | classroom   la classe | to climb   escalader |

Fifi est au cinéma.
Fifi is at the cinema.

La classe est vide.
The classroom is empty.

Sam escalade la falaise.
Sam is climbing the cliff.

| circle   le cercle | clean   propre | clock   l'horloge (f) |

Les poussins* forment un cercle.
The chicks are in a circle.

Bill met un tablier propre.
Bill puts on a clean apron.

Ben nettoie l'horloge.
Ben is cleaning the clock.

| circus   le cirque | to clean   nettoyer | to close   fermer |

Un clown au cirque.
A clown at the circus.

Henri nettoie sa voiture.
Henry cleans his car.

Fifi ferme la fenêtre.
Fifi closes the window.

cloud   **le nuage**

L'ange est sur un nuage.
The angel is on a cloud.

clown   **le clown**

Un clown du cirque.
A clown from the circus.

coach   **le car**

Un car plein de clowns.
A coach full of clowns.

coast   **la côte**

Des arbres poussent le long de la côte.
Trees grow along the coast.

coat   **le manteau**

Le roi a un long manteau.
The king has a long coat.

cobweb   **la toile d'araignée**

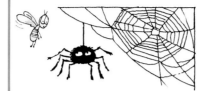

Voici une toile d'araignée.
Here is a cobweb.

cockerel   **le coq**

Le coq chante.
The cockerel is calling.

coffee   **le café**

Fifi verse le café.
Fifi pours the coffee.

coin   **la pièce**

Fifi met les pièces* dans son porte-monnaie.
Fifi puts the coins in her purse.

cold   **froid**

Oscar a froid.
Oscar is cold.

colour   **la couleur**

Combien de couleurs* vois-tu?
How many colours can you see?

comb   **le peigne**

Fifi a un grand peigne.
Fifi has a big comb.

to comb   **se peigner**

Fifi se peigne.
Fifi combs her hair.

to come   **venir**

Le canard vient vers Mimi.
The duck comes to Mimi.

comic   **l'illustré (m)**

Les garçons lisent un illustré.
The boys are reading a comic.

computer l'ordinateur (m)	corn le blé	to count compter

Brains travaille sur un ordinateur.
Brains works on a computer.

Du blé pousse dans le champ.
Corn is growing in the field.

Mimi compte les gâteaux.
Mimi is counting the cakes.

conductor le chef d'orchestre	corner le coin	country le pays

Herbert est chef d'orchestre.
Herbert is a conductor.

Ruff est au coin.
Ruff is in the corner.

L'Angleterre est un petit pays; la Chine et l'Inde sont de grands pays. *
England is a small country; China and India are big countries.

to cook faire la cuisine	to cost coûter	country la campagne

Henri fait la cuisine.
Henry is cooking.

Cette bague coûte mille francs.
This ring costs 1000 francs.

Dan vit à la campagne.
Dan lives in the country.

cooker la cuisinière	cotton le coton	to cover couvrir

Sa cuisinière est très ancienne.
His cooker is very old.

Fifi coud avec du fil de coton.
Fifi is sewing with cotton thread.

Bill se couvre la tête.
Bill covers his head.

cork le bouchon	to cough tousser	cow la vache

Le bouchon saute.
The cork pops up.

Fifi tousse.
Fifi is coughing.

Une poule sur une vache.
A hen on a cow.

cowboy	**le cowboy**

Un cowboy poursuit une vache.
A cowboy chases a cow.

crab	**le crabe**

Un crabe court de travers.
A crab runs sideways.

crane	**la grue**

La grue soulève la voiture.
The crane is lifting the car.

crayon	**le crayon de couleur**

Mimi dessine avec des crayons* de couleur.
Mimi draws with crayons.

cream	**la crème**

Il y a de la crème sur ce gâteau.
There is cream on this cake.

crocodile	**le crocodile**

Le crocodile dort.
The crocodile is asleep.

cross	**la croix**

Trois souris sur une croix rouge.
Three mice on a red cross.

to cross	**traverser**

Henri traverse la rue.
Henry crosses the road.

crossroads	**le carrefour**

Il s'arrête au carrefour.
He stops at the crossroads.

crown	**la couronne**

Le roi porte une couronne.
The king wears a crown.

to cry	**pleurer**

Le roi pleure.
The king is crying.

cube	**le cube**

Un cube a six côtés.
A cube has six sides.

cucumber	**le concombre**

Le concombre est vert.
The cucumber is green.

cup	**la tasse**

La chenille regarde dans la tasse.
The caterpillar looks in the cup.

cupboard	**le placard**

La tasse est dans le placard.
The cup is in the cupboard.

curtain	le rideau

Fifi ouvre les rideaux.
Fifi opens the curtains.

dark	sombre

La pièce est sombre.
The room is dark.

cushion	le coussin

La couronne est sur un coussin.
The crown is on a cushion.

to dance	danser

Fifi danse avec Sam.
Fifi is dancing with Sam.

daughter	la fille

Mimi est la fille de Mary.
Mimi is Mary's daughter.

customer	le client

Un client achète du pain.
A customer buys bread.

dancer	la danseuse[1]

Elle veut être danseuse.
She wants to be a dancer.

day	le jour

Il y a 365 jours* dans l'année.
There are 365 days in a year.

Il y a sept jours* dans la semaine.
There are seven days in a week.

to cut	couper

Fifi coupe les cheveux de Ben.
Fifi cuts Ben's hair.

danger	le danger

Henri est en danger.
Henry is in danger.

dead	mort

Max fait semblant d'être mort.
Max pretends to be dead.

to cut out	découper

Elle découpe une image.
She cuts out a picture.

to dare	oser

Il n'ose pas plonger.
He does not dare dive.

to decide	décider

Bill décide d'acheter une voiture.
Bill decides to buy a car.

Décide quelle robe tu veux.
Decide which dress you want.

22   1. male dancer: **le danseur**

| deep | **profond** | desk | **le bureau** | to dig | **creuser** |

Fifi est en eau profonde.
Fifi is in deep water.

Jake travaille à son bureau.
Jake works at his desk.

Max creuse un trou.
Max is digging a hole.

| deer | **le cerf** | diamond | **le diamant** | dining room | **la salle à manger** |

Max rencontre un cerf.
Max meets a deer.

Fred trouve un diamant.
Fred finds a diamond.

Les souris mangent dans la salle à manger.
The mice eat in the dining room.

| dentist | **le dentiste** | dictionary | **le dictionnaire** | dinner | **le dîner** |

Henri va chez le dentiste.
Henry visits the dentist.

Fritz a un dictionnaire.
Fritz has a dictionary.

Le monstre mange son dîner.
The monster is eating his dinner.

| to describe | **décrire** | to die | **mourir** | dinosaur | **le dinosaure** |

Bill décrit le voleur à la police.
Bill describes the thief to the police.

Peux-tu décrire cette image?
Can you describe this picture?

La plante est en train de mourir.
The plant is dying.

Le dinosaure mange son dîner.
The dinosaur is eating his dinner.

| desert | **le désert** | different | **différent** | direction | **la direction** |

Les chameaux vivent dans le désert.
Camels live in the desert.

Deux chapeaux différents.
Two different hats.

Max change de direction.
Max changes direction.

dirty	sale	doll	la poupée	to draw	dessiner

Le dinosaure est sale.
The dinosaur is dirty.

Mimi joue avec sa poupée.
Mimi plays with her doll.

Fifi dessine un dragon.
Fifi is drawing a dragon.

dish	le plat	donkey	l'âne (m)	drawing	le dessin

Un plat rempli de fraises.
A dish full of strawberries.

Henri est monté sur un âne.
Henry is riding a donkey.

Voici son dessin.
Here is her drawing.

to do	faire	door	la porte	to dream	rêver

Henri ne fait rien.
Henry is doing nothing.

Fifi ferme la porte.
Fifi shuts the door.

Henri rêve d'araignées.
Henry dreams about spiders.

doctor	le médecin	downstairs	en bas	dress	la robe

Le médecin examine Sam.
The doctor examines Sam.

La poupée est en bas.
The doll is downstairs.

Fifi porte une robe longue.
Fifi is wearing a long dress.

dog	le chien	dragon	le dragon	to dress	habiller

Le chien poursuit un lapin.
The dog chases a rabbit.

Le dragon crache du feu.
The dragon breathes fire.

Fifi habille Mimi.
Fifi is dressing Mimi.

to drink	**boire**

Sam boit du lait.
Sam is drinking milk.

to drive	**conduire**

Henri conduit sa voiture.
Henry is driving his car.

to drop	**laisser tomber**

Henri laisse tomber un oeuf.
Henry drops an egg.

drum	**le tambour**

Fred joue du tambour.
Fred is playing the drum.

dry	**sec, sèche**

Le sol est très sec.
The ground is very dry.

duck	**le canard**

Le canard est dans la baignoire.
The duck is in the bath.

dust	**la poussière**

Max se roule dans la poussière.
Max rolls in the dust.

dustbin	**la poubelle**

Bill regarde dans la poubelle.
Bill looks in the dustbin.

duvet	**la couette**

Fifi a une couette rose.
Fifi has a pink duvet.

each	**chaque**

Chaque enfant a un gâteau.
Each child has a cake.

eagle	**l'aigle (m)**

L'aigle est dans son nid.
The eagle is in its nest.

ear	**l'oreille (f)**

L'âne a de longues oreilles. *
The donkey has long ears.

early	**tôt**

Ben se lève tôt le matin.
Ben gets up early in the morning.

Je reviendrai tôt.
I am coming home early.

earth	**la terre**

La Terre est ronde.
The Earth is round.

25

| east | l'est (m) | egg | l'oeuf (m) | end | le bout |

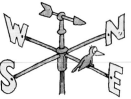

L'oiseau est orienté à l'est.
The bird is facing east.

Mimi mange un oeuf.
Mimi is eating an egg.

La souris se balance au bout de la corde.
The mouse is at the end of the rope.

| Easter | Pâques (m) | elbow | le coude | enough | assez |

Pâques est une fête religieuse.
Easter is a religious holiday.

Les gens ne travaillent pas le lundi de Pâques.
People don't work on Easter Monday.

Henri se cogne le coude.
Henry hits his elbow.

Fifi a assez d'argent pour acheter une nouvelle voiture.
Fifi has enough money to buy a new car.

As-tu assez mangé?
Have you had enough to eat?

| easy | facile | elephant | l'éléphant (m) | to enter | entrer |

Ce gâteau est facile à faire.
This cake is easy to make.

Les devoirs de Sam sont faciles.
Sam's homework is easy.

Un éléphant a de grandes oreilles.
An elephant has big ears.

Le roi entre dans la pièce.
The king enters the room.

| to eat | manger | empty | vide | entrance | l'entrée (f) |

Mimi mange du chocolat.
Mimi is eating chocolate.

Le sac est vide.
The bag is empty.

L'entrée de la caverne.
The entrance to the cave.

| edge | le bord | to empty | vider | envelope | l'enveloppe (f) |

Mimi est au bord de la table.
Mimi is on the edge of the table.

Henri vide le seau.
Henry empties the bucket.

Fifi ouvre l'enveloppe.
Fifi opens the envelope.

to escape	**s'évader**

Le prisonnier s'évade.
The prisoner escapes.

evening	**le soir**

Le soleil se couche le soir.
The sun sets in the evening.

every	**tous, toutes**

Tous les cochons sont roses.
Every pig is pink.

everyone	**tout le monde**

Tout le monde porte un chapeau.
Everyone is wearing a hat.

everything	**tout**

Tout est vert.
Everything is green.

---

everywhere	**partout**

Fifi cherche son chat partout.
Fifi looks everywhere for her cat.

Mon chien me suit partout.
My dog follows me everywhere.

except	**sauf**

Tous les cochons sont roses sauf un.
Every pig is pink except one.

exciting	**passionnant**

Jake lit un livre passionnant.
Jake reads an exciting book.

exercise book	**le cahier**

Tim écrit dans son cahier.
Tim is writing in his exercise book.

experiment	**l'expérience**

Brains fait une expérience.
Brains does an experiment.

---

to explain	**expliquer**

Fifi explique pourquoi elle veut une voiture.
Fifi explains why she wants a car.

Explique-moi comment cela marche.
Explain to me how this works.

eyes	**les yeux**[1]

Le chat a les yeux* bleus.
The cat has blue eyes.

face	**la figure**

Fifi se lave la figure.
Fifi washes her face.

factory	**l'usine**

Bill travaille dans une usine.
Bill works in a factory.

---

1. eye (singular): **l'oeil (m)**

fair	**blond**	far	**loin**	father	**le père**

L'ami de Fifi a les cheveux blonds.
Fifi's friend has fair hair.

La maison est loin.
The house is far away.

Mimi est avec son père.
Mimi is with her father.

fairy	**la fée**	farm	**la ferme**	feather	**la plume**

La fée est assise sur une fleur.
The fairy sits on a flower.

La ferme est à la campagne.
The farm is in the country.

Un oiseau à plumes jaunes.
A bird with yellow feathers.

to fall	**tomber**	farmer	**le fermier**	to feed	**nourrir**

La fée tombe.
The fairy falls off.

Le fermier vit à la ferme.
The farmer lives on the farm.

Mimi nourrit les canards.
Mimi feeds the ducks.

family	**la famille**	fast	**vite**	to feel	**toucher**

Une famille de fées.
A family of fairies.

Le fermier court vite.
The farmer runs fast.

Bill touche la chaise.
Bill can feel the chair.

famous	**célèbre**	fat	**gros, grosse**	feet	**les pieds (m)***

Will est un peintre célèbre.
Will is a famous artist.

Cette fée est grosse.
This fairy is fat.

Voici deux grands pieds.*
Here are two big feet.

| fence | **la clôture** | film | **le film** | fireman | **le pompier** |

La vache saute par-dessus la clôture.
The cow jumps over the fence.

Fifi et Sam regardent un film.
Fifi and Sam watch a film.

Les pompiers* éteignent le feu.
The firemen put out the fire.

| few | **peu** | to find | **trouver** | fireworks | **le feu d'artifice**[1] |

Cet oiseau a peu de plumes.*
This bird has few feathers.

Bill trouve son livre.
Bill finds his book.

Un feu d'artifice dans le ciel.
Fireworks in the sky.

| field | **le champ** | finger | **le doigt** | first | **premier, première** |

Les vaches sont dans un champ.
The cows are in a field.

Quatre doigts* et un pouce.
Four fingers and a thumb.

Bill est le premier de la file.
Bill is first in the queue.

| to fight | **se battre** | to finish | **finir** | fish | **le poisson** |

Bill et Ben se battent.
Bill and Ben are fighting.

Fifi finit son dîner.
Fifi finishes her dinner.

Un gros poisson et un petit poisson.
A big fish and a little fish.

| to fill | **remplir** | fire | **le feu** | to fish | **pêcher à la ligne** |

Fifi remplit le verre.
Fifi fills the glass.

Ces hommes sont assis près du feu.
These men sit by the fire.

Tim pêche à la ligne.
Tim is fishing.

---

1. The word for 'fireworks' is always singular in French.

flag **le drapeau**	flour **la farine**	fog **le brouillard**

Henri porte un drapeau.
Henry is carrying a flag.

Bill tamise la farine.
Bill is sieving the flour.

Henri est perdu dans le brouillard.
Henry is lost in the fog.

flame **la flamme**	to flow **couler**	to follow **suivre**

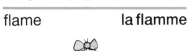

Mimi souffle sur la flamme.
Mimi blows out the flame.

La rivière coule vers la mer.
The river flows towards the sea.

Henri suit un chien.
Henry is following a dog.

flat **plat**	flower **la fleur**	food **la nourriture**

Cette maison a un toit plat.
This house has a flat roof.

Henri donne une fleur à Fifi.
Henry gives Fifi a flower.

Une assiette pleine de nourriture.
A plate full of food.

flat **l'appartement (m)**	fly **la mouche**	football **le ballon de football**

Fifi habite dans un appartement.
Fifi lives in a flat.

Il y a une mouche sur la fleur.
There is a fly on the flower.

Sam donne un coup de pied dans le ballon de football.
Sam kicks the football.

floor **le plancher**	to fly **voler**	for **pour**

Ruff est couché sur le plancher.
Ruff is lying on the floor.

La mouche vole.
The fly is flying.

Ce cadeau est pour Ben.
This present is for Ben.

forehead	le front

Henri se cogne le front.
Henry hits his forehead.

forest	la forêt

Il y a beaucoup d'arbres dans une forêt.
There are many trees in a forest.

to forget	oublier

Bill a oublié mon nom.
Bill has forgotten my name.

Ne m'oubliez pas!
Don't forget me!

J'ai oublié où il habite.
I have forgotten where he lives.

fork	la fourchette

Ben tient une fourchette.
Ben is holding a fork.

fox	le renard

Le renard est roux.
The fox is red.

to freeze	geler

Quand l'eau gèle, elle se transforme en glace.
When water freezes it turns into ice.

	congeler

Fifi congèle les aliments au congélateur.
Fifi freezes food in the freezer.

fridge	le réfrigérateur

Ben met du lait dans le réfrigérateur.
Ben puts milk in the fridge.

friend	l'ami (m)

Sam et Fifi sont amis. *
Sam and Fifi are friends.

to frighten	faire peur à

Fifi fait peur à son ami.
Fifi frightens her friend.

frog	la grenouille

La grenouille saute.
The frog is jumping.

from	de

Cette lettre vient de France.
This letter is from France.

Elle est de Pierre et elle est adressée à Fifi.
It is from Pierre to Fifi.

Je vais au cinéma de temps en temps.
I go to the cinema from time to time.

in front of	devant

Ben est devant Bill.
Ben is in front of Bill.

frost	le gel

Il y a du gel sur la vitre.
There is frost on the window.

fruit	le fruit

Plusieurs sortes de fruits.
Many kinds of fruit.

fry	faire cuire[1]

Bill fait cuire un oeuf sur le plat.[1]
Bill fries an egg.

---

1. **faire cuire** means 'to cook'. The word **frire** (to fry) is only used when talking about frying fish.

frying pan	la poêle	game	le jeu	to get up	se lever

Des oeufs cuisant dans une poêle.
Eggs frying in a frying pan.

Un jeu de colin-maillard.
A game of blindman's buff.

Ben se lève à sept heures.
Ben gets up at 7 o'clock.

full	plein	garage	le garage	ghost	le fantôme

La baignoire est pleine d'eau.
The bath is full of water.

La voiture est dans le garage.
The car is in the garage.

Le fantôme fait peur à Henri.
The ghost frightens Henry.

funny	drôle	garden	le jardin	giant	le géant

Le clown est drôle.
The clown is funny.

Des fleurs poussent dans le jardin.
Flowers grow in the garden.

Un géant est un homme très grand.
A giant is a very big man.

fur	la fourrure	gas	le gaz	giraffe	la girafe

Le lapin a une fourrure blanche.
The rabbit has white fur.

Henri allume le gaz.
Henry lights the gas.

La girafe mange des feuilles.
The giraffe is eating leaves.

	gate	la barrière	girl	la fille

Le fermier ferme la barrière.
The farmer shuts the gate.

La petite fille poursuit le chat.
The little girl chases the cat.

to give	donner	goat	la chèvre	grapefruit	le pample-mousse

L'enfant donne une fleur à Ben.
The child gives Ben a flower.

La chèvre mord Henri.
The goat bites Henry.

Fifi mange un pamplemousse.
Fifi eats a grapefruit.

glass	le verre	gold	l'or (m)	grass	l'herbe (f)

Le verre est plein de lait.
The glass is full of milk.

Fifi a une chaîne d'or.
Fifi has a gold chain.

Ruff se roule dans l'herbe.
Ruff is rolling in the grass.

glasses	les lunettes (f)	good	bon, bonne	green	vert

Henri porte des lunettes. *
Henry is wearing glasses.

Ben est un bon boulanger.
Ben is a good baker.

L'herbe est verte.
The grass is green.

glove	le gant	goose	l'oie (f)	grey	gris

Une paire de gants* rouges.
A pair of red gloves.

L'oie poursuit la chèvre.
The goose chases the goat.

Le gros chat est gris.
The big cat is grey.

to go	aller	grape	le raisin	grocer	l'épicier (m)

Les enfants vont en classe.
The children go to school.

Voici une grappe de raisin.
Here is a bunch of grapes.

Voici l'épicier.
Here is the grocer.

33

ground le sol	gun le pistolet	half la moitié

Mimi est assise sur le sol.
Mimi is sitting on the ground.

Sam tire au pistolet.
Sam shoots the gun.

Mimi a une moitié d'orange.
Mimi has half an orange.

---

group   **le groupe**

ham   **le jambon**

Voici un groupe de garçons.
Here is a group of boys.

Bill coupe le jambon.
Bill is cutting the ham.

---

to grow   **grandir**

hair   **les cheveux (m)**[1]

hammer   **le marteau**

Mimi grandit.
Mimi is growing.

Mamie a les cheveux blancs.
Nan has white hair.

Henri se sert d'un marteau.
Henry is using a hammer.

---

guest   **l'invité**

hairbrush   **la brosse à cheveux**

hand   **la main**

Fifi accueille son invité.
Fifi welcomes her guest.

Mamie a une brosse à cheveux rose.
Nan has a pink hairbrush.

Henri se cogne la main.
Henry hits his hand.

---

guitar   **la guitare**

hairdresser   **le coiffeur**

handbag   **le sac à main**

Manuel joue de la guitare.
Manuel is playing the guitar.

Le coiffeur coupe les cheveux de Fifi.
The hairdresser cuts Fifi's hair.

Fifi a un sac à main rouge.
Fifi has a red handbag.

handkerchief	le mouchoir

Fifi agite son mouchoir.
Fifi waves her handkerchief.

handle	l'anse (f)²

L'anse casse.
The handle breaks.

to hang	suspendre

Henri est suspendu à une corde.
Henry is hanging from a rope.

to happen	se passer

Que se passe-t-il?
What is happening?

arriver

Quand l'accident est-il arrivé?
When did the accident happen?

Comment cela est-il arrivé?
How did it happen?

happy	content

Bill est content de voir Ben.
Bill is happy to see Ben.

harbour	le port

Les bateaux sont dans le port.
The boats are in the harbour.

hard	dur

Ce matelas est dur.
This mattress is hard.

hat	le chapeau

Fifi porte un joli chapeau.
Fifi is wearing a pretty hat.

to have	avoir³

Bill et Ben ont deux chats.
Bill and Ben have two cats.

hay	le foin

Gilles coupe l'herbe pour faire du foin.
Giles cuts grass to make hay.

head	la tête

Henri a un oiseau sur la tête.
Henry has a bird on his head.

headlights	les phares (f)

Les phares* éclairent.
The headlights are shining.

to hear	entendre

Le vieil homme n'entend pas bien.
The old man cannot hear well.

heart	le coeur

Quand tu cours, ton coeur bat plus vite.
When you run, your heart beats faster.

Je t'aime de tout mon coeur.
I love you with all my heart.

Je connais cette chanson par coeur.
I know this song by heart.

heavy	lourd

Cette pierre est lourde.
This rock is heavy.

2. **L'anse** is only used to mean the handle of a cup.   3. See page 83.

hedge	la haie

Henri taille la haie.
Henry is cutting the hedge.

here	ici

Je reste ici.
I am staying here.

Viens ici.
Come here.

voici

Voici notre maison.
Here is our house.

hippopotamus	l'hippopotame (m)

Un hippopotame plein de boue.
A muddy hippopotamus.

hedgehog	le hérisson

Voici un hérisson.
Here is a hedgehog.

to hide	se cacher

Le voleur se cache.
The thief is hiding.

to hit	frapper

Mimi frappe Ruff.
Mimi hits Ruff.

helicopter	l'hélicoptère (m)

L'hélicoptère vole.
The helicopter is flying.

high	haut

Voici une haute montagne.
This is a high mountain.

to hold	tenir

La sorcière tient un balai.
The witch is holding a broom.

to help	aider

Bill aide Ben.
Bill is helping Ben.

high	haut

L'oiseau vole haut dans le ciel.
The bird flies high in the sky.

hole	le trou

Ruff creuse un trou.
Ruff is digging a hole.

hen	la poule

La poule mange des graines.
The hen is eating seeds.

hill	la colline

La maison est sur une colline.
The house is on a hill.

holiday	les vacances (f)[1]

Bill est en vacances.
Bill is on holiday.

1. The word for 'holiday' is always plural in French.

homework les devoirs (m)[2]	hot chaud	how comment

homework les devoirs (m)[2]

Tim fait ses devoirs.
Tim is doing his homework.

hot chaud

La soupe est chaude.
The soup is hot.

how comment

Comment vas-tu?
How are you?

Comment fait-on un gâteau?
How do you make a cake?

Comment dit-on cela en français?
How do you say it in French?

honey le miel

Le miel est dans le pot.
The honey is in the jar.

hotel l'hôtel (m)

Fifi va à l'hôtel.
Fifi is going to a hotel.

to be hungry avoir faim

Mimi a faim.
Mimi is hungry.

hook le crochet

Le chapeau est suspendu à un crochet.
The hat is hanging on a hook.

hour l'heure (f)

Il y a 24 heures* dans une journée.
There are 24 hours in a day.

Il y a 60 minutes dans une heure.
There are 60 minutes in an hour.

to hurry se dépêcher

Henri se dépêche.
Henry is hurrying.

horse le cheval

Henri monte à cheval.
Henry is riding a horse.

house la maison

Fritz habite dans une grande maison.
Fritz lives in a big house.

husband le mari

Fritz est le mari de Heidi.
Fritz is Heidi's husband.

hospital l'hôpital (m)

Henri est à l'hôpital.
Henry is in hospital.

hovercraft l'aéroglisseur (m)

Un aéroglisseur va vite.
A hovercraft goes fast.

hut la cabane

L'ouvrier est dans la cabane.
The workman is in the hut.

2. The word for 'homework' is always plural.

Ii

ill   **malade**

Bill est malade.
Bill is ill.

to invite   **inviter**

Fifi a invité 20 personnes à sa fête.
Fifi has invited 20 people to her party.

---

ice   **la glace**

La mare est couverte de glace.
The pond is covered in ice.

important   **important**

Le Premier Ministre est un personnage important.
The Prime Minister is an important person.

C'est très important.
It is very important.

iron   **le fer à repasser**

Voici un fer à repasser.
This is an iron.

---

ice cream   **la glace**

Mimi mange une glace.
Mimi is eating an ice cream.

in   **dans**

Le chat est dans son panier.
The cat is in its basket.

to iron   **repasser**

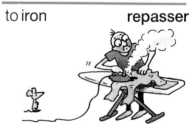

Henri repasse sa chemise.
Henry is ironing his shirt.

---

idea   **l'idée (f)**

Quelle bonne idée!
What a good idea!

Je viens d'avoir une idée.
I have had an idea.

Je n'ai pas la moindre idée.
I have not the least idea.

insect   **l'insecte (m)**

Voici des insectes. *
These are insects.

island   **l'île (f)**

Une île dans la mer.
An island in the sea.

---

if   **si**

Viens si tu peux.
Come if you can.

Fifi demande si Sam est à la maison.
Fifi asks if Sam is at home.

Il t'aidera si tu lui demandes.
He will help you if you ask him.

instead of   **au lieu de**

Fifi mange du miel au lieu de manger du sucre.
Fifi eats honey instead of sugar.

Il joue au lieu de travailler.
He is playing instead of working.

Jj

jacket	**la veste**

Fritz a une veste verte.
Fritz has a green jacket.

jam	**la confiture**

Un pot de confiture de fraises.
A jar of strawberry jam.

jar	**le bocal**

Voici un bocal vide.
This is an empty jar.

jeans	**le blue-jean**

Voici un blue-jean.
This is a pair of jeans.

jewel	**le bijou**

Le cambrioleur aperçoit les bijoux.*
The burglar sees the jewels.

to join	**attacher**

Bill attache deux fils.
Bill joins two wires.

joke	**la plaisanterie**

Bill raconte une plaisanterie.
Bill tells a joke.

jug	**la cruche**

Fifi verse le lait de la cruche.
Fifi pours the milk from the jug.

to jump	**sauter**

Une grenouille saute.
One frog is jumping.

kangaroo	**le kangourou**

Le kangourou saute.
The kangaroo is jumping.

to keep	**garder**

Fifi veut garder la robe.
Fifi wants to keep the dress.

Ben garde sa vieille voiture.
Ben is keeping his old car.

Garde du pain pour demain.
Keep some bread for tomorrow.

kennel	**la niche**

Ruff dort dans une niche.
Ruff sleeps in a kennel.

kettle	**la bouilloire**

La bouilloire bout.
The kettle is boiling.

key	**la clé**

La clé est suspendue à un crochet.
The key is on a hook.

to kick   donner un coup de pied

Sam donne un coup de pied dans le ballon.
Sam kicks the ball.

to kill   tuer

Le prince a tué le dragon.
The prince has killed the dragon.

kind   bon, bonne

Jim est bon envers les animaux.
Jim is kind to animals.

kind   la sorte

Une pomme est une sorte de fruit.
An apple is a kind of fruit.

Un oignon est une sorte de légume.
An onion is a kind of vegetable.

C'est quelle sorte de gâteau?
What kind of cake is it?

king   le roi

Le roi porte une couronne.
The king is wearing a crown.

to kiss   embrasser

Fifi embrasse Sam.
Fifi is kissing Sam.

kitchen   la cuisine

Ben est dans la cuisine.
Ben is in the kitchen.

kite   le cerf-volant

Bill joue avec un cerf-volant.
Bill is playing with a kite.

kitten   le chaton

Un chaton est un bébé chat.
A kitten is a baby cat.

knee   le genou

Henri tombe sur son genou.
Henry falls on his knee.

knife   le couteau

Bill coupe du pain avec un couteau.
Bill cuts bread with a knife.

to knit   tricoter

Henri tricote.
Henry is knitting.

knitting   le tricot

Voici son tricot.
This is his knitting.

to knock   frapper

Sam frappe à la porte.
Sam knocks at the door.

knot   le noeud

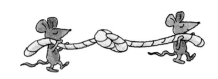

Il y a un noeud dans la ficelle.
The string has a knot in it.

to know — savoir[1]

Fritz sait nager.
Fritz knows how to swim.

Je sais que deux et deux font quatre.
I know that two and two make four.

connaître[2]

Sam connaît Ben.
Sam knows Ben.

lace — la dentelle

Cette robe est en dentelle.
This dress is made of lace.

ladder — l'échelle (f)

Henri monte à l'échelle.
Henry climbs the ladder.

lake — le lac

Il y a des bateaux sur le lac.
There are boats on the lake.

lamb — l'agneau (m)

Un agneau est un bébé mouton.
A lamb is a baby sheep.

lamp — la lampe

Fifi lit à la lumière de la lampe.
Fifi is reading by the lamp.

last — dernier, dernière

Ben est le dernier de la file.
Ben is the last in the queue.

to last — durer

Le film dure une heure.
The film lasts an hour.

Le beau temps a duré cinq jours.
The good weather lasted for five days.

Combien de temps cela va t-il durer?
How long will it last?

late — en retard

Tim est en retard.
Tim is late.

tard

Il se couche tard.
He goes to bed late.

Est-ce trop tard pour le film?
Am I too late for the film?

to laugh — rire

Ben rit.
Ben is laughing.

lawn — le gazon

Fifi tond le gazon.
Fifi is mowing the lawn.

lazy — paresseux

Tim est paresseux.
Tim is lazy.

to lead — mener

Ben mène les enfants.
Ben is leading the children.

lead — la laisse

Le chien est en laisse.
The dog is on a lead.

---

1. Used for facts and things.   2. Used for people.

| leaf | la feuille | leek | le poireau | letter | la lettre |

La fourmi transporte une feuille.
The ant is carrying a leaf.

Les souris transportent un poireau.
The mice are carrying a leek.

Sam lit une lettre.
Sam is reading a letter.

| to lean | s'appuyer | left | gauche | lettuce | la laitue |

Bruno s'appuie contre la clôture.
Bruno is leaning on the fence.

Fritz tourne à gauche.
Fritz turns left.

La chenille aime la laitue.
The caterpillar likes lettuce.

| to learn | apprendre | leg | la jambe | library | la bibliothèque |

Fifi apprend à conduire.
Fifi is learning how to drive.

J'apprends le français à l'école.
I am learning French at school.

Henri patine sur une jambe.
Henry is skating on one leg.

Bill est dans la bibliothèque.
Bill is in the library.

| leather | le cuir | lemon | le citron | to lick | lécher |

Ce sac est en cuir.
This bag is made of leather.

Fifi coupe un citron en deux.
Fifi cuts a lemon in half.

Mimi lèche sa glace.
Mimi licks her ice cream.

| to leave | quitter | lesson | la leçon | lid | la couvercle |

Fifi quitte la maison.
Fifi is leaving the house.

Les élèves ont une leçon.
The pupils are having a lesson.

Bill met le couvercle sur le bocal.
Bill puts the lid on the jar.

42

life	**la vie**

Les papillons ont la vie courte.
Butterflies have a short life.

La vie est très tranquille ici.
Life is very quiet here.

Il m'a sauvé la vie.
He saved my life.

lift	**l'ascenseur (m)**

Henri entre dans l'ascenseur.
Henry enters the lift.

to lift	**soulever**

La grue soulève une voiture.
The crane is lifting a car.

light	**léger, légère**

La danseuse est légère.
The dancer is light.

light	**la lumière**

La lumière est allumée.
The light is on.

to light	**allumer**

Fritz allume une allumette.
Fritz lights a match.

lighthouse	**la phare**

Le phare est sur la côte.
The lighthouse is on the coast.

lightning	**l'éclair (m)**

L'éclair illumine le ciel.
Lightning flashes in the sky.

to like	**aimer bien**

Fifi aime bien Ben.
Fifi likes Ben.

line	**la rangée**

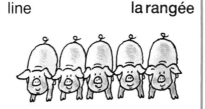

Une rangée de cinq cochons.
Five pigs in a line.

lion	**le lion**

Le lion rugit.
The lion is roaring.

lip	**la lèvre**

Des grosses lèvres* rouges.
Big red lips.

list	**la liste**

Henri fait une longue liste.
Henry makes a long list.

to listen	**écouter**

Papy écoute la radio.
Pop listens to the radio.

to live	**vivre**

Rob vit sur une île.
Rob lives on an island.

long   **long, longue**

Le serpent est long.
The snake is long.

to look at   **regarder**

Fifi regarde un tableau.
Fifi is looking at a picture.

to look for   **chercher**

Henri cherche un livre.
Henry is looking for a book.

lorry   **le camion**

Henri conduit un camion.
Henry is driving a lorry.

lost   **égaré**

Henri s'est égaré.
Henry is lost.

a lot of   **beaucoup de**

Il y a beaucoup d'oiseaux dans l'arbre.
A lot of birds in a tree.

loud   **bruyant**

La fanfare est bruyante.
The band is loud.

to love   **aimer**

Sam aime Fifi.
Sam loves Fifi.

low   **bas, basse**

Le mur est bas.
The wall is low.

to have lunch   **déjeuner**

Mimi déjeune.
Mimi has lunch.

machine   **la machine**

Toutes ces machines* marchent.
All these machines work.

magazine   **la revue**

Henri lit une revue.
Henry is reading a magazine.

magician:le prestidigitateur

Voici un prestidigitateur.
Here is a magician.

to make   **faire**

Ben fait un gâteau.
Ben is making a cake.

man	l'homme (m)	to marry	épouser	medicine	le médicament

Un homme et deux femmes.
One man and two women.

Sam épouse Fifi.
Sam is marrying Fifi.

L'infirmière donne un médicament à Mimi.
The nurse gives Mimi medicine.

---

many	beaucoup de	mask	le masque	to meet	rencontrer

Beaucoup de revues* à vendre.
Many magazines for sale.

Qui porte le masque?
Who is wearing the mask?

Bill rencontre Ben.
Bill meets Ben.

---

map	la carte	match	l'allumette (f)	to melt	fondre

Henri regarde une carte.
Henry looks at a map.

Fred allume une allumette.
Fred lights a match.

La glace fond.
The ice cream is melting.

---

mark	la tache	to measure	mesurer	to mend	réparer

Il y a une tache sur la carte.
There is a mark on the map.

Fifi mesure Mimi.
Fifi measures Mimi.

Ben répare sa bicyclette.
Ben is mending his bicycle.

---

market	le marché	meat	la viande	menu	le menu

Voici un marché.
This is a market.

Le boucher coupe de la viande.
The butcher is chopping meat.

Fifi lit le menu.
Fifi reads the menu.

metal	**le métal**

Une voiture est faite de métal.
A car is made of metal.

middle	**le milieu**

Le cochon est au milieu des chèvres.
The pig is in the middle of the goats.

milk	**le lait**

Mimi boit du lait.
Mimi is drinking milk.

minute	**la minute**

Il y a 60 secondes dans une minute.
There are 60 seconds in a minute.

Il y a 60 minutes* dans une heure.
There are 60 minutes in an hour.

mirror	**la glace**

Le chat regarde dans la glace.
The cat looks in the mirror.

to miss	**rater**

Henri a raté l'autobus.
Henry has missed the bus.

model	**le modèle réduit**

Fritz fait un modèle réduit d'avion.
Fritz is making a model aeroplane.

money	**l'argent (m)**

Ben compte son argent.
Ben is counting his money.

monkey	**le singe**

Le singe se balance.
The monkey is swinging.

monster	**le monstre**

Le monstre est aimable.
The monster is friendly.

month	**le mois**

Il y a douze mois* dans l'année.
There are twelve months in the year.

Janvier est le premier mois de l'année.
January is the first month of the year.

Décembre est le dernier.
December is the last month.

moon	**la lune**

La lune est dans le ciel.
The moon is in the sky.

more	**plus**

Bill a plus d'argent que Ben.
Bill has more money than Ben.

morning	**le matin**

Avant midi, c'est le matin.
Morning comes before midday.

Nous nous levons le matin.
We get up in the morning.

Le matin, les gens vont au travail et les enfants à l'école.
In the morning people go to work and children go to school.

most	**la plupart**

La plupart des pommes sont rouges.
Most of the apples are red.

| mother   **la mère** | mouth   **la bouche** | music   **la musique** |

Mary est la mère de Mimi.
Mary is Mimi's mother.

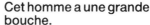

Cet homme a une grande bouche.
This man has a big mouth.

La fanfare joue de la musique.
The band plays music.

---

motorbike   **la moto**

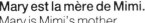

Henri conduit une moto.
Henry is riding a motorbike.

to move   **déplacer**

Ils déplacent la table.
They are moving the table.

---

mountain   **la montagne**

Voici une haute montagne.
This is a high mountain.

much   **beaucoup**

As-tu beaucoup d'argent?
Have you much money?

Je me sens beaucoup mieux.
I feel much better.

A-t-il eu beaucoup de succès?
Has he had much success?

nail   **le clou**

Henri tape sur un clou.
Henry hits a nail.

---

mouse   **la souris**

Une des souris* est rose.
One of the mice is pink.

mud   **la boue**

Le monstre joue dans la boue.
The monster is playing in the mud.

name   **le nom**

Mimi écrit son nom.
Mimi writes her name.

---

moustache   **la moustache**

Cet homme a une moustache.
This man has a moustache.

mushroom   **le champignon**

Une souris sur un champignon.
A mouse on a mushroom.

naughty   **vilain**

Mimi est vilaine.
Mimi is naughty.

near **près de**	nest **le nid**	night **la nuit**

L'arbre est près de la maison.
The tree is near the house.

Les oisillons vivent dans un nid.
Baby birds live in a nest.

Il fait nuit.
It is night.

neck **le cou**	never **ne . . . jamais**	nobody **personne**

Une girafe a un long cou.
A giraffe has a long neck.

Fifi ne mange jamais de fromage.
Fifi never eats cheese.

Je ne regarde jamais la télévision.
I never watch television.

Papy ne sort jamais.
Pop never goes out.

Personne ne porte de chapeau.
Nobody is wearing a hat.

necklace **le collier**	new **nouveau, nouvelle**	noise **le bruit**

Fifi porte un collier.
Fifi is wearing a necklace.

Ben a une nouvelle voiture.
Ben has a new car.

Mimi fait du bruit.
Mimi is making a noise.

to need **avoir besoin de**	newspaper **le journal**	north **le nord**

Mimi a besoin d'un bain.
Mimi needs a bath.

Bill lit le journal.
Bill reads the newspaper.

L'oiseau est orienté au nord.
The bird is facing north.

needle **l'aiguille (f)**	next to **à côté de**	nose **le nez**

Fifi enfile une aiguille.
Fifi threads a needle.

Fifi est assise à côté de Sam.
Fifi is sitting next to Sam.

Henri a le nez rouge.
Henry has a red nose.

| notebook | le carnet | nurse | l'infirmière (f) | office | le bureau |

L'homme consulte son carnet.
The man looks at his notebook.

Une infirmière donne un médicament à Ben.
A nurse gives Ben medicine.

Jake travaille dans un bureau.
Jake works in an office.

| nothing | rien | nut | la noix | often | souvent |

Il n'y a rien dans la boîte.
There is nothing in the box.

Mimi mange des noix.*
Mimi is eating nuts.

Le téléphone sonne souvent.
The telephone often rings.

| notice | l'écriteau (m) | | | to oil | huiler |

Fred lit un écriteau.
Fred is reading a notice.

Tim huile sa bicyclette.
Tim oils his bicycle.

| now | maintenant | octopus | la pieuvre | old | vieux, vieille |

Il est maintenant cinq heures.
It is now 5 o'clock.

Je dois partir maintenant.
I must go now.

Maintenant je rentre à la maison.
Now I am going home.

Voici une pieuvre.
Here is an octopus.

Papy est un vieux monsieur.
Pop is an old man.

| number | le nombre | to offer | offrir | on | sur |

Voici des nombres.*
Here are some numbers.

Sam offre des fleurs à Fifi.
Sam offers Fifi flowers.

La tasse est sur la table.
The cup is on the table.

onion **l'oignon (m)**

Henri coupe un oignon.
Henry is slicing an onion.

only **seulement**

Un cochon seulement est noir.
Only one pig is black.

to open **ouvrir**

Fifi ouvre la porte.
Fifi opens the door.

open **ouvert**

Le magasin est ouvert.
The shop is open.

opposite **en face de**

Ben est assis en face de Bill.
Ben is sitting opposite Bill.

or **ou**

Quelles chaussures veux-tu, les bleues ou les rouges?
Which shoes do you want, the blue ones or the red ones?

Tu peux avoir l'une ou l'autre paire.
You can have one pair or the other.

orange **orange**

Henri a des chaussettes orange.
Henry has orange socks.

orange **l'orange (f)**

Une orange est orange.
An orange is orange.

to order **commander**

Fritz commande son dîner.
Fritz orders dinner.

other **autre**

Où est l'autre chaussette?
Where is the other sock?

out of **hors de**

Les jouets sont hors de la boîte.
The toys are out of the box.

outside **dehors**

Mimi joue dehors.
Mimi is playing outside.

over **par-dessus**

Le cochon saute par-dessus la clôture.
The pig jumps over the fence.

owl **le hibou**

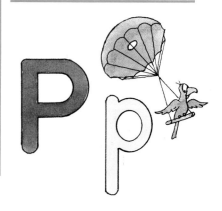

Le hibou est dans l'arbre.
The owl is in the tree.

P p

| page | **la page** | pancake | **la crêpe** | park | **le parc** |

Voici la première page.
This is the first page.

Bill fait des crêpes. *
Bill is making pancakes.

Fifi se promène dans le parc.
Fifi is walking in the park.

---

to **paint**   **peindre**

L'artiste peint.
The artist is painting.

paper   **le papier**

Fifi peint sur du papier.
Fifi is painting on paper.

to **park**   **garer**

Henri gare sa voiture.
Henry is parking his car.

---

paints   **les couleurs (f)**

Voici ses couleurs. *
These are her paints.

parachute   **le parachute**

Le parachute descend.
The parachute is coming down.

parrot   **le perroquet**

Le perroquet rit.
The parrot is laughing.

---

pair   **la paire**

Une paire de chaussettes orange.
A pair of orange socks.

parcel   **le paquet**

Le facteur apporte un paquet.
The postman brings a parcel.

party   **la fête**

C'est la fête de Fifi.
It is Fifi's party.

---

palace   **le palais**

Le roi vit dans un palais.
The king lives in a palace.

parents   **les parents (m)** *

Mimi est avec ses parents. *
Mimi is with her parents.

to **pass**   **passer devant**

Henri passe devant Bruno.
Henry passes Bruno.

passport	**le passeport**

Ben montre son passeport.
Ben shows his passport.

path	**le chemin**

Le chemin passe à travers champs.
The path crosses the field.

patient	**le malade**

Le malade est au lit.
The patient is in bed.

pavement	**le trottoir**

Fifi est sur le trottoir.
Fifi is on the pavement.

paw	**la patte**

Le chat se lèche la patte.
The cat is licking its paw.

to pay	**payer**

Fifi paie le boulanger.
Fifi pays the baker.

peach	**la pêche**

Bill mange une pêche.
Bill is eating a peach.

pear	**la poire**

Ben mange une poire.
Ben is eating a pear.

pea	**le petit pois**

Mimi mange des petits pois. *
Mimi is eating peas.

pen	**le stylo**

Fifi écrit avec un stylo.
Fifi writes with a pen.

pencil	**le crayon**

Elle dessine avec un crayon.
She draws with a pencil.

people	**les gens (m)[1]**

Ces gens* parlent.
These people are talking.

pepper	**le poivre**

Bill met du poivre dans son assiette.
Bill puts pepper on his plate.

perhaps	**peut-être**

Il va peut-être pleuvoir.
Perhaps it will rain.

Il s'est peut-être perdu.
Perhaps he is lost.

petrol	**l'essence (f)**

Henri met de l'essence dans sa voiture.
Henry puts petrol in his car.

| photograph | **la photo** | picture | **le tableau** | pillow | **l'oreiller (m)** |

Voici une photo de Fifi.
This is a photograph of Fifi.

Un tableau représentant un pique-nique.
A picture of a picnic.

Mimi a un oreiller moelleux.
Mimi has a soft pillow.

| piano | **le piano** | pie | **la tarte** | pilot | **le pilote** |

Fritz joue du piano.
Fritz plays the piano.

Bill coupe la tarte.
Bill cuts the pie.

Un pilote aux commandes d'un avion.
A pilot flying an aeroplane.

| to pick | **cueillir** | piece | **le morceau** | pin | **l'épingle (f)** |

Les gens cueillent des poires. *
The people are picking pears.

Mimi mange un morceau de tarte.
Mimi eats a piece of pie.

Bill pique Ben avec une épingle.
Bill pricks Ben with a pin.

| to pick up | **ramasser** | pig | **le cochon** | to pinch | **pincer** |

Fifi ramasse une poire.
Fifi picks up a pear.

Voici un cochon rose.
This is a pink pig.

Bill pince Ben.
Bill pinches Ben.

| picnic | **le pique-nique** | pile | **la pile** | pineapple | **l'ananas (m)** |

Les amis font un pique-nique.
The friends have a picnic.

Henri a une pile de livres.
Henry has a pile of books.

Un gros ananas.
A big pineapple.

pink	rose

Le gros cochon est rose.
The big pig is pink.

pipe	la pipe

Ben fume la pipe.
Ben is smoking a pipe.

place	l'endroit (m)

Ben cherche un endroit où pique-niquer.
Ben is looking for a place to have a picnic.

Elle habite un joli endroit.
She lives in a pretty place.

plant	la plante

Henri tient une plante.
Henry holds a plant.

to plant	planter

Il la plante dans le jardin.
He plants it in the garden.

plate	l'assiette (f)

Les frites sont dans une assiette.
The chips are on a plate.

to play	jouer

Les enfants jouent.
The children are playing.

pocket	la poche

Le mouchoir est dans la poche.
The handkerchief is in the pocket.

to point	montrer du doigt

Ben montre Bill du doigt.
Ben is pointing at Bill.

policeman	le gendarme

Le gendarme montre Bill du doigt.
The policeman is pointing at Bill.

to polish	cirer

Fritz cire la table.
Fritz is polishing the table.

polite	poli

Bill est très poli.
Bill is very polite.

Il est poli de dire s'il vous plaît quand on demande quelque chose.
It is polite to say please when you ask for something.

pond	la mare

Des canards nagent sur la mare.
Ducks are swimming on a pond.

pony	le poney

Henri monte un poney.
Henry is riding a pony.

poor	pauvre

Un homme pauvre a peu d'argent.
A poor man has little money.

| pork | le porc | post office | la poste | to pretend | faire semblant de |

Fritz mange du porc.
Fritz is eating pork.

Fifi est à la poste.
Fifi is at the post office.

Fifi fait semblant d'être un fantôme.
Fifi pretends to be a ghost.

| port | le port | potato | la pomme de terre | pretty | joli, jolie |

Le bateau est dans le port.
The ship is in the port.

Henri épluche une pomme de terre.
Henry peels a potato.

Fifi est une jolie fille.
Fifi is a pretty girl.

| porter | le porteur | to pour | verser | price | le prix |

Un porteur porte des valises
A porter carries cases.

Henri verse du vin.
Henry is pouring wine.

Quel est le prix des pommes de terre?
What is the price of the potatoes?

| postcard | la carte postale | pram | le landau | prize | le prix |

Fifi écrit une carte postale.
Fifi writes a postcard.

Mimi est dans un landau.
Mimi is in a pram.

Henri a gagné un prix.
Henry has won a prize.

| postman | le facteur | present | le cadeau | to promise | promettre |

Le facteur apporte des lettres.
The postman brings letters.

Henri donne un cadeau à Fifi.
Henry gives Fifi a present.

Fifi a promis d'envoyer une carte postale à Henri.
Fifi has promised to send Henry a postcard.

Je promets de venir.
I promise I will come.

pudding	le dessert	purse	le porte-monnaie	

Mimi aime les desserts.
Mimi likes puddings.

Fifi met de l'argent dans son porte-monnaie.
Fifi puts money in her purse.

---

to pull — **tirer**

Bill et Ben tirent sur la corde.
Bill and Ben are pulling the rope.

to push — **pousser**

Bill pousse Ben.
Bill is pushing Ben.

queen — **la reine**

La reine porte une couronne.
The queen wears a crown.

---

puppet — **la marionnette**

La marionnette danse.
The puppet is dancing.

to put — **mettre**

Fifi met du lait dans le réfrigérateur.
Fifi puts milk in the fridge.

question — **la question**

La reine pose une question au roi.
The queen asks the king a question.

Réponds à ma question.
Answer my question.

La question est sans réponse.
The question has no answer.

---

puppy — **le chiot**

Un chiot est un bébé chien.
A puppy is a baby dog.

puzzle — **le puzzle**

Fritz fait un puzzle.
Fritz is doing a puzzle.

queue — **la queue**

Henri fait la queue.
Henry is standing in a queue.

---

purple — **pourpre**

Le roi a un manteau pourpre.
The king has a purple coat.

pyjamas — **le pyjama**[1]

Henri porte un pyjama.
Henry is wearing pyjamas.

quietly — **silencieusement**

Le cambrioleur avance silencieusement.
The burglar is walking quietly.

---

1. This word is used in the singular.

quite	assez

Le film est assez bon, mais le livre est meilleur.
The film is quite good but the book is better.

Il est assez intelligent.
He is quite clever.

rabbit	le lapin

Le lapin court.
The rabbit is running.

race	la course

Les lapins font la course.
The rabbits are having a race.

radiator	le radiateur

Un radiateur chauffe la pièce.
A radiator heats a room.

radio	la radio

Papy écoute la radio.
Pop is listening to the radio.

railway line	la voie ferrée

Un lapin est sur la voie ferrée.
A rabbit is on the railway line.

to rain	pleuvoir

Il pleut.
It is raining.

rainbow	l'arc-en-ciel

Voici un arc-en-ciel.
Here is a rainbow.

raincoat	l'imperméable (m)

Henri porte un imperméable.
Henry is wearing a raincoat.

raspberry	la framboise

Un plat de framboises. *
A dish of raspberries.

rat	le rat

Le rat poursuit un lapin.
The rat is chasing a rabbit.

razor	le rasoir

Sam se rase avec un rasoir.
Sam shaves with a razor.

to reach	atteindre

Fifi ne peut pas atteindre le livre.
Fifi cannot reach the book.

to read	lire

Fifi lit un livre.
Fifi is reading a book.

| real   **vrai** | to refuse   **refuser** | rich   **riche** |

Voici un vrai éléphant.
This is a real elephant.

L'âne refuse de bouger.
The donkey refuses to move.

Voici un homme riche.
This is a rich man.

---

to **receive**   **recevoir**

Fifi reçoit une lettre.
Fifi receives a letter.

to remember   **se souvenir de** / **se rappeler de**

Fritz se souvient de Fifi.
Fritz remembers Fifi.

Henri ne se rappelle plus où il a mis son livre.
Henry cannot remember where he put his book.

to **ride**   **monter**

Henri monte sur un âne.
Henry is riding a donkey.

---

to **recognise**   **reconnaître**

Fritz reconnaît Fifi.
Fritz recognizes Fifi.

Je reconnais son écriture.
I recognize her writing.

to **rest**   **se reposer**

Henri se repose.
Henry is resting.

right   **droit**

Fifi lève la main droite.
Fifi raises her right hand.

---

record   **le disque**

Bill met un disque.
Bill puts on a record.

ribbon   **le ruban**

Mimi a un ruban bleu dans les cheveux.
Mimi has a blue ribbon in her hair.

ring   **la bague**

Une bague à la main droite.
A ring on a right hand.

---

red   **rouge**

Fifi peint la chaise en rouge.
Fifi is painting the chair red.

rice   **le riz**

Wong Fu mange du riz.
Wong Fu is eating rice.

to **ring**   **sonner**

Le téléphone sonne.
The telephone is ringing.

river **la rivière**	room **la pièce**	round **rond**

La rivière est large.
The river is wide.

Voici une pièce de la maison.
This is a room in the house.

La table est ronde.
The table is round.

road **la route**	root **la racine**	row **le rang**

Il y a des moutons sur la route.
There are sheep on the road.

Cette plante a de longues racines. *
This plant has long roots.

Les fleurs sont en rang.
The flowers are in a row.

to roar **rugir**	rope **la corde**	to row **ramer**

Le lion rugit.
The lion is roaring.

Henri grimpe à une corde.
Henry is climbing a rope.

Bill rame.
Bill is rowing.

rock **le rocher**	rose **la rose**	to rub **se frotter**

Henri est assis sur un rocher.
Henry is sitting on a rock.

La rose sent bon.
The rose smells sweet.

Le chat se frotte le dos.
The cat is rubbing its back.

roof **le toit**	rough **mauvais**	to run **courir**

La maison a un toit rouge.
The house has a red roof.

La route est mauvaise.
The road is rough.

Henri court.
Henry is running.

sack — le sac

Le voleur porte un grand sac.
The thief is carrying a big sack.

sad — triste

Henri est triste.
Henry is sad.

safe — sain et sauf

Henri est sain et sauf.
Henry is safe.

to sail — faire du voilier

Fifi fait du voilier.
Fifi is sailing.

sailor — le marin

Un marin sur son bateau.
A sailor on his boat.

salad — la salade

Voici une salade.
Here is a salad.

salt — le sel

Bill met du sel sur la salade.
Bill puts salt on the salad.

same — même

Deux filles portant le même chapeau.
Two girls in the same hat.

sand — le sable

Mimi creuse un trou dans le sable.
Mimi is digging in the sand.

sandal — la sandale

Une paire de sandales. *
A pair of sandals.

sandwich — le sandwich

Un très gros sandwich.
A very big sandwich.

satchel — le cartable

Tim a un cartable rouge.
Tim has a red satchel.

sauce — la sauce

Fifi verse la sauce.
Fifi is pouring the sauce.

saucepan — la casserole

Ben prend la casserole.
Ben picks up the saucepan.

saucer	la soucoupe	scarf	l'écharpe (f)	seal	le phoque

Henri a une très longue écharpe.
Henry has a very long scarf.

Le phoque est dans la mer.
The seal is in the sea.

La tasse est sur la soucoupe.
The cup is on the saucer.

sausage	la saucisse	school	l'école (f)	to see	voir

Ben mange des saucisses. *
Ben is eating sausages.

Les enfants sont à l'école.
The children are at school.

Mimi voit le phoque.
Mimi can see the seal.

saw	la scie	scissors	les ciseaux (m) *	seed	la graine

Bill coupe du bois avec une scie.
Bill cuts wood with a saw.

Fifi se sert de ciseaux. *
Fifi is using scissors.

Dan plante des graines. *
Dan is planting seeds.

to say	dire	to scratch	se gratter	to seem	sembler

Bill dit qu'il est riche.
Bill says he is rich.

Leur lettre dit qu'ils vont bien.
The letter says they are well.

Elle dit qu'ils vont venir.
She says they are coming.

Ruff se gratte l'oreille.
Ruff is scratching his ear.

Il semble être en colère.
He seems to be angry.

scales	la balance	sea	la mer	to sell	vendre

Fifi est debout sur la balance.
Fifi stands on the scales.

La mer est bleue.
The sea is blue.

Le boulanger vend du pain.
The baker sells bread.

to send **envoyer**	shadow **l'ombre (f)**	sharp **aiguisé**

Fifi envoie une lettre.
Fifi is sending a letter.

Mimi regarde son ombre.
Mimi is looking at her shadow.

Le couteau est aiguisé.
The knife is sharp.

sentence **la phrase**	to shake **secouer**	sheep **le mouton**

Voici une phrase.
This is a sentence.

Bill secoue l'arbre.
Bill is shaking the tree.

Trois moutons* en rang.
Three sheep in a row.

to serve **servir**	shape **la forme**	sheet **le drap**

Le garçon sert Fifi.
The waiter is serving Fifi.

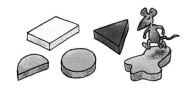

Voici différentes formes.*
These are different shapes.

Fifi met un drap sur le lit.
Fifi puts a sheet on the bed.

to sew **coudre**	to share **partager**	shell **le coquillage**

Henri coud.
Henry is sewing.

Bill et Ben partagent le gâteau.
Bill and Ben share the cake.

Mimi ramasse un coquillage.
Mimi picks up a shell.

sewing machine **la machine à coudre**	shark **le requin**	ship **le navire**

Il se sert d'une machine à coudre.
He is using a sewing machine.

Le requin poursuit Henri.
The shark is chasing Henry.

Le navire est en mer.
The ship is at sea.

shirt **la chemise**	shoulder **l'épaule (f)**	side **le côté**

Fritz a une chemise bleue.
Fritz has a blue shirt.

Il y a un oiseau sur l'épaule de Bob.
A bird is on Bob's shoulder.

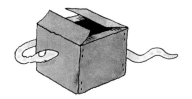

Un côté de la boîte est rose.
One side of the box is pink.

---

shoe **la chaussure**	to shout **crier**	silver **l'argent (m)**[2]

Une paire de chaussures* rouges.
A pair of red shoes.

Ben crie.
Ben is shouting.

Fifi a un bracelet d'argent.
Fifi has a silver bracelet.

---

shop **le magasin**	to show **montrer**	since **depuis**

Fifi n'a pas vu Ben depuis mardi.
Fifi has not seen Ben since Tuesday.

Fifi entre dans un magasin.
Fifi goes into a shop.

Fifi montre son dessin à Papy.
Fifi shows Pop her picture.

puisque

Puisqu'il fait beau, je vais me promener.
Since it is sunny, I will go for a walk.

---

short **court**	shower **la douche**	to sing **chanter**

Le serpent jaune est court.
The yellow snake is short.

Henri prend une douche.
Henry is having a shower.

Les gens chantent.
The people are singing.

---

shorts **le short**[1]	shut **fermé**	sister **la soeur**

Henri porte un short blanc.
Henry is wearing white shorts.

La barrière est fermée.
The gate is shut.

Mimi et Daisy sont soeurs.*
Mimi and Daisy are sisters.

---

1. This word is used in the singular.   2. This is also the word for 'money'.   63

to sit	être assis

Mimi est assise sur une chaise.
Mimi is sitting on a chair.

sitting room	le salon

Voici un salon.
This is a sitting room.

to skate	patiner

Fifi et Henri patinent.
Fifi and Henry are skating.

ski	le ski

Henri met des skis.*
Henry puts on skis.

to ski	faire du ski

Henri fait du ski.
Henry is skiing.

skin	la peau

Un éléphant a la peau grise.
An elephant has grey skin.

skirt	la jupe

Fifi porte une jupe rouge.
Fifi is wearing a red skirt.

sky	le ciel

L'oiseau est dans le ciel.
The bird is in the sky.

to sleep	dormir

Mimi dort.
Mimi is sleeping.

sleeve	la manche

Cette chemise n'a qu'une manche.
This shirt only has one sleeve.

slice	la tranche

Bill coupe une tranche de pain.
Bill cuts a slice of bread.

to slide	glisser

Henri glisse sur la glace.
Henry is sliding on the ice.

slide	la diapositive

Voici une diapositive.
This is a slide.

slipper	la pantoufle

Mimi a des pantoufles* rouges.
Mimi has red slippers.

slowly	lentement

Un escargot avance lentement.
A snail moves slowly.

64

small petit	snake le serpent	soft moelleux, moelleuse

L'ours brun est petit.
The brown bear is small.

Le serpent est dans l'herbe.
The snake is in the grass.

Le coussin est moelleux.
The cushion is soft.

---

to smell **sentir**	to snow **neiger**	soldier **le soldat**

Fifi sent l'odeur du parfum.
Fifi smells the perfume.

Il neige.
It is snowing.

Un soldat est dans l'armée.
A soldier is in the army.

---

to smile **sourire**	soap **le savon**	some **certain**

Fifi sourit.
Fifi is smiling.

Ben a du savon sur la figure.
Ben has soap on his face.

Certains soldats sourient.
Some soldiers are smiling.

---

to smoke **fumer**	sock **la chaussette**	someone **quelqu'un**

Quelqu'un a volé ma voiture.
Someone has stolen my car.

something   quelque chose

J'ai quelque chose dans l'oeil.
There is something in my eye.

sometimes   quelquefois

Papy fume la pipe.
Pop is smoking a pipe.

Mimi porte des chaussettes* roses.
Mimi is wearing pink socks.

Quelquefois je suis triste.
Sometimes I am sad.

---

snail l'escargot (m)	sofa **le canapé**	son **le fils**

Re-voici l'escargot.
Here is the snail again.

Fifi est assise sur le canapé.
Fifi is sitting on the sofa.

Henri est le fils de Papy.
Henry is Pop's son.

| song | la chanson | space | l'espace (m) | spider | l'araignée (f) |

La chanteuse chante une chanson.
The singer is singing a song.

L'astronaute est dans l'espace.
The astronaut is in space.

L'araignée fait peur à Fifi.
The spider frightens Fifi.

| soon | bientôt | spade | la pelle | spoon | la cuiller |

Nous rentrerons bientôt à la maison.
We will go home soon.

A bientôt!
I'll see you soon!

Dan bêche avec une pelle.
Dan is digging with a spade.

Mimi mange avec une cuiller.
Mimi is eating with a spoon.

| sort | la sorte | to speak | parler | spot | le bouton |

Trois sortes* de chapeaux.
Three sorts of hat.

Fifi parle à Papy.
Fifi is speaking to Pop.

Mimi a beaucoup de boutons.*
Mimi has lots of spots.

| soup | la soupe | to spell | épeler | to spread | étaler |

Henri mange de la soupe.
Henry is eating soup.

Mimi sait épeler son nom.
Mimi can spell her name.

Bill étale le beurre.
Bill is spreading the butter.

| south | le sud | to spend | dépenser | square | le carré |

L'oiseau est orienté au sud.
The bird is facing South.

Ben dépense de l'argent.
Ben is spending money.

Voici un carré.
This is a square.

stable	l'écurie (f)	to start	commencer	stem	la tige

Le cheval vit dans une écurie.
The horse lives in a stable.

La course commence.
The race is starting.

La fleur a une longue tige.
The flower has a long stem.

stairs	l'escalier (m)[1]	station	la gare	step	la marche

Mimi monte l'escalier.
Mimi is going up the stairs.

Le train est en gare.
The train is in the station.

Le chat est assis sur les marches. *
The cat is sitting on the steps.

stamp	le timbre	statue	la statue	stereo	la chaîne stéréo

Deux timbres * **sur une enveloppe.**
Two stamps on an envelope.

Henri regarde une statue.
Henry is looking at a statue.

Voici une chaîne stéréo.
This is a stereo.

to stand	se tenir debout	to stay	rester	stick	le bâton

Bill se tient debout sur le dos de Ben.
Bill is standing on Ben's back.

Reste ici!
Stay here!

Fifi reste au lit.
Fifi stays in bed.

Henri doit rester quatre jours à Paris.
Henry is staying in Paris for 4 days.

Dan porte des bâtons. *
Dan is carrying sticks.

star	l'étoile (f)	to steal	voler	stockings	les bas (m)

L'étoile brille dans le ciel.
The star shines in the sky.

Fred vole des bijoux.
Fred is stealing jewels.

Fifi a des bas * **noirs.**
Fifi has black stockings.

stone	**la pierre**

Mimi ramasse une pierre.
Mimi picks up a stone.

to stop	**s'arrêter**

La voiture s'arrête au feu rouge.
The car stops at the lights.

storm	**l'orage (m)**

Voici un orage.
This is a storm.

story	**l'histoire (f)**

Papy lit une histoire.
Pop is reading a story.

straight	**droit**

The road is straight.
La route est droite.

strawberry	**la fraise**

Mimi mange une fraise.
Mimi is eating a strawberry.

stream	**le ruisseau**

Fifi traverse un ruisseau.
Fifi is crossing a stream.

street	**la rue**

Voici une rue.
This is a street.

string	**la ficelle**

Un bout de ficelle.
A piece of string.

striped	**rayé**

Fifi porte une robe rayée.
Fifi has a striped dress.

strong	**fort**

Sam est fort.
Sam is strong.

stupid	**bête**

Henri se sent bête.
Henry feels stupid.

submarine	**le sous-marin**

Le sous-marin est en plongée.
The submarine is underwater.

suddenly	**brusquement**

La voiture s'arrête brusquement.
The car stops suddenly.

sugar	**le sucre**

Fifi met du sucre dans son thé.
Fifi puts sugar in her tea.

suit	le costume

Henri porte un costume.
Henry is wearing a suit.

suitcase	la valise

Ben porte une valise.
Ben is carrying a suitcase.

sun	le soleil

Le soleil brille.
The sun is shining.

supermarket	le supermarché

Fifi est au supermarché.
Fifi is at the supermarket.

surprise	la surprise

Une surprise pour Fifi.
A surprise for Fifi.

to surround	entourer

Les oiseaux entourent le chat.
The birds surround the cat.

to swallow	avaler

Le serpent avale quelque chose.
The snake swallows something.

swan	le cygne

Le cygne nage.
The swan is swimming.

sweet	le bonbon

Mimi mange des bonbons. *
Mimi is eating sweets.

to swim	nager

Bill et Ben nagent.
Bill and Ben are swimming.

swimsuit	le maillot de bain

Fifi a un maillot de bain rayé.
Fifi has a striped swimsuit.

swimming pool	la piscine

Voici la piscine.
This is the swimming pool.

swing	la balançoire

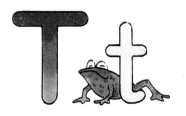

Ben est sur une balançoire.
Ben is on a swing.

table	la table

Le chat est sur la table.
The cat is on the table.

tail	la queue	taxi	le taxi	to tear	déchirer

Un seul chat a une queue.
Only one cat has a tail.

Fritz appelle un taxi.
Fritz calls a taxi.

Henri déchire son pantalon.
Henry tears his trousers.

tall	grand	tea	le thé	tear	la larme

La dame est grande.
The woman is tall.

Fifi prend une tasse de thé.
Fifi has a cup of tea.

Mimi a des larmes* sur la figure.
Mimi has tears on her face.

to take	prendre	teacher	le professeur	teddy bear	l'ours en peluche (m)

Mimi prend un chocolat.
Mimi takes a chocolate.

Le professeur fait la classe.
The teacher is teaching the class.

Mimi a un ours en peluche.
Mimi has a teddy bear.

tap	le robinet	team	l'équipe (f)	teeth	les dents (m)

La souris ouvre le robinet.
The mouse turns on the tap.

Une équipe de football.
A football team.

Le rat a des dents* pointues.
The rat has sharp teeth.

to taste	goûter	teapot	la théière	telephone	le téléphone

Ben goûte la sauce.
Ben is tasting the sauce.

Fifi verse du thé d'une théière.
Fifi pours tea from a teapot.

Le téléphone sonne.
The telephone is ringing.

television	la télévision

Les enfants regardent la télévision.
The children are watching television.

to tell	raconter

Papy raconte une histoire aux enfants.
Pop is telling the children a story.

tennis	le tennis

Ces hommes jouent au tennis.
These men are playing tennis.

tent	la tente

Henri met la tête hors de la tente.
Henry looks out of the tent.

to thank	remercier

Fifi remercie Ben de son cadeau.
Fifi thanks Ben for the present.

that	ce, cette, cet[1]

Donne-moi ce chapeau.
Give me that hat.
Donne-moi cette pomme.
Give me that apple.

that is	voilà

Voilà ma soeur!
That is my sister!
Voilà mon frère!
That is my brother!

theatre	le théâtre

Fifi est au théatre.
Fifi is at the theatre.

then	puis

Il a dîné, puis il a mangé un morceau de gâteau.
He ate his dinner, then he had a piece of cake.

Mets un timbre sur la lettre, puis poste-la.
Put a stamp on the letter, then post it.

there	là

Est-ce que Fifi est là?
Is Fifi there?

Ne bouge pas de là.
Do not move from there.

thick	épais, épaisse

La tranche de pain est épaisse.
The slice of bread is thick.

thief	le voleur

Le voleur vole des bijoux.
The thief is stealing jewels.

thin	maigre

Cet homme est maigre.
This man is thin.

thing	la chose

Plusieurs choses* sur un plateau.
Several things on a tray.

to think	penser

Fifi pense à Sam.
Fifi is thinking about Sam.

to be thirsty	avoir soif

Cet homme a soif.
This man is thirsty.

71

this	ce, cette, cet[1]

Prends ce chapeau.
Take this hat.

this is	voici

Voici un éléphant.
This is an elephant.

through	par

Le roi entre par la porte.
The king comes in through the door.

to throw	jeter

Mimi jette du pain aux canards.
Mimi is throwing bread to the ducks.

thumb	le pouce

Henri se tape sur le pouce.
Henry hits his thumb.

ticket	le billet

Fifi montre son billet.
Fifi shows her ticket.

tie	la cravate

Henri a une cravate à pois.
Henry has a spotted tie.

to tie (a knot)	faire un noeud

Bill fait un noeud.
Bill is tying a knot.

tiger	le tigre

Le tigre rugit.
The tiger is roaring.

tights	le collant[2]

Un collant rouge.
Red tights.

tired	fatigué

Henri est fatigué.
Henry is tired.

to	à

Les enfants vont à l'école.
The children go to school.

Henri va à la gare.
Henry is going to the station.

Bill donne une pomme à Ben.
Bill gives an apple to Ben.

today	aujourd'hui

Aujourd'hui, c'est l'anniversaire de Mimi.
Today is Mimi's birthday.

toe	le doigt de pied

La souris chatouille les doigts de pied* de Sam.
The mouse is tickling Sam's toes.

together	ensemble

Les chats dorment ensemble.
The cats sleep together.

tomato	la tomate

Henri coupe des tomates.*
Henry is slicing tomatoes.

1. See page 82.   2. This word is used in the singular.

| tomorrow | **demain** | toothpaste | **le dentifrice** | tower | **la tour** |

**Demain est le jour qui suit
aujourd'hui.**
Tomorrow is the day after today.

**Aujourd'hui c'est lundi, alors
demain ce sera mardi.**
Today is Monday so tomorrow will
be Tuesday.

**Du dentifrice sur une brosse à
dents.**
Toothpaste on a toothbrush.

Où se trouve cette célèbre tour?
Where is this famous tower?

| tongue | **la langue** | top | **le haut** | town | **la ville** |

Ruff a une langue rose.
Ruff has a pink tongue.

Ben est en haut de l'escabeau.
Ben is at the top of the steps.

Voici une ville.
This is a town.

| too | **trop** | to touch | **toucher** | toy | **le jouet** |

La veste est trop petite.
The jacket is too small.

Qui touche l'épaule du voleur?
Who touches the thief's shoulder?

Mimi s'amuse avec un jouet.
Mimi is playing with a toy.

| tool | **l'outil (m)** | towards | **vers** | tractor | **le tracteur** |

Voici des outils. *
Here are some tools.

Le chat se dirige vers son lait.
The cat goes towards his milk.

Henri conduit un tracteur.
Henry is driving a tractor.

| toothbrush | **la brosse à dents** | towel | **la serviette** | traffic lights | **les feux** |

Une brosse à dents jaune.
A yellow toothbrush.

Henri a une serviette jaune.
Henry has a yellow towel.

**Il est rentré dans le panneau des
feux.**
He has hit the traffic lights.

| train | **le train** | trumpet | **la trompette** | tyre | **le pneu** |

Henri monte dans un train.
Henry gets on a train.

Ben joue de la trompette.
Ben is playing a trumpet.

Les pneus* de la bicyclette sont à plat.
The bicycle has flat tyres.

| treasure | **le trésor** | tulip | **la tulipe** | twin | **la jumelle**[2] |

Ali Baba trouve un trésor.
Ali Baba finds treasure.

Les tulipes sont dans un vase.
The tulips are in a vase.

Bella et Betty sont jumelles.*
Bella and Betty are twins.

| tree | **l'arbre** | to turn | **tourner** |

L'arbre a des feuilles vertes.
The tree has green leaves.

La voiture tourne à droite.
The car is turning left.

| triangle | **le triangle** | to type | **taper à la machine** | ugly | **laid** |

Ce sont des triangles.*
These are triangles.

Henri tape à la machine.
Henry is typing.

Le monstre est laid.
The monster is ugly.

| trousers | **le pantalon**[1] | typewriter | **la machine à écrire** | umbrella | **le parapluie** |

Ben porte un pantalon rouge.
Ben has red trousers.

La machine à écrire est vieille.
The typewriter is old.

Henri perd son parapluie.
Henry loses his umbrella.

74   1. This word is used in the singular.   2. Male twin; **le jumeau.**

uncle	l'oncle (m)

Tom est l'oncle de Mimi.
Tom is Mimi's uncle.

under	sous

Le chat est sous le lit.
The cat is under the bed.

underground	le métro

Une station de métro.
An underground station.

to understand	comprendre

Je comprends ce qu'il dit.
I understand what he says.

Je comprends comment fonctionne cette machine.
I understand how this machine works.

Je comprends le français.
I understand French.

to undress	déshabiller

Fifi déshabille Mimi.
Fifi is undressing Mimi.

unhappy	mécontent

Henri est mécontent.
Henry is unhappy.

until	jusqu'à

Attends jusqu'à dix heures.
Wait until ten o'clock.

Il travaille jusqu'au soir.
He works until the evening.

to go up	monter

Henri monte à une échelle.
Henry is going up a ladder.

upstairs	en haut

Le chat est en haut.
The cat is upstairs.

to use	se servir de

Fifi se sert d'un couteau.
Fifi uses a knife.

useful	utile

Un couteau, c'est utile.
A knife is useful.

vacuum cleaner	l'aspirateur (m)

Un aspirateur rouge.
A red vacuum cleaner.

valley	la vallée

Une rivière dans une vallée.
A river in a valley.

van	la camionnette

Henri conduit une camionnette.
Henry is driving a van.

| vase — **le vase** | to visit — **rendre visite à** | to wake up — **se réveiller** |

Le vase est plein de fleurs.
The vase is full of flowers.

Fifi rend visite à Papy.
Fifi is visiting Pop.

Henri se réveille.
Henry is waking up.

---

vegetable — **le légume**

Voici des légumes. *
Here are some vegetables.

voice — **la voix**

Papy a une voix douce.
Pop has a quiet voice.

Ben a la voix grave et Fifi a la voix aigüe.
Ben has a low voice and Fifi has a high voice.

wall — **le mur**

Les chats sont sur le mur.
The cats are on the wall.

---

very — **très**

La jeune fille est très jolie.
The girl is very pretty.

Henri parle très bien français.
Henry speaks French very well.

Très bien!
Very good!

wallpaper — **le papier peint**

Bill pose du papier peint.
Bill is putting up wallpaper.

---

village — **le village**

Un village est une petite ville.
A village is a small town.

to wait — **attendre**

Aggie attend l'autobus.
Aggie is waiting for the bus.

walk — **la promenade**

Fifi fait une promenade.
Fifi is going for a walk.

---

violin — **le violon**

Henri joue du violon.
Henry plays the violin.

waiter — **le garçon**

Le garçon sert Fifi.
The waiter serves Fifi.

to want — **vouloir**

Mimi veut un gâteau.
Mimi wants a cake.

war	la guerre

Ces deux pays sont en guerre.
The two countries are at war.

La guerre a duré deux ans.
The war has lasted two years.

washing machine	la machine à laver

La machine à laver est en marche.
The washing machine is on.

wave	la vague

Ben plonge sous la vague.
Ben dives under the wave.

wardrobe	l'armoire (f)

Fifi regarde dans l'armoire.
Fifi looks in the wardrobe.

wasp	la guêpe

La guêpe a piqué Henri.
The wasp has stung Henry.

weak	faible

Henri est faible.
Henry is weak.

warm	chaud

Fifi a chaud.
Fifi is warm.

watch	la montre

Fifi regarde sa montre.
Fifi looks at her watch.

to wear	porter

Fifi porte un chapeau.
Fifi is wearing a hat.

to wash	se laver

Henri se lave la figure.
Henry is washing his face.

water	l'eau (f)

La baignoire est pleine d'eau.
The bath is full of water.

wedding	le mariage

Un mariage à l'église.
A wedding at the church.

wash basin	le lavabo

Le lavabo est jaune.
The wash basin is yellow.

waterfall	la chute d'eau

Tarzan franchit la chute d'eau.
Tarzan crosses the waterfall.

to weigh	peser

Fifi pèse la farine.
Fifi weighs the flour.

| west | l'ouest (m) | where | où | white | blanc, blanche |

L'oiseau est orienté à l'ouest.
The bird is facing west.

Où est le chat?
Where is the cat?

Le gros chat est blanc.
The fat cat is white.

| wet | mouillé | which | quel, quelle | who | qui |

Le chien est mouillé.
The dog is wet.

Quel est le plus gros chat?
Which cat is the biggest?

Qui porte un chapeau?
Who is wearing a hat?

| wheel | la roue | while | pendant | why | pourquoi |

Une bicyclette a deux roues.
A bicycle has two wheels.

Mimi rêve pendant son sommeil.
Mimi dreams while she sleeps.

Pourquoi Henri est-il dans l'arbre?
Why is Henry up a tree?

| wheelbarrow | la brouette | to whisper | chuchoter | wide | large |

La brouette est pleine.
The wheelbarrow is full.

Fifi chuchote quelque chose à Ben.
Fifi is whispering to Ben.

La rivière est très large.
The river is very wide.

| when | quand | whistle | le sifflet | wife | la femme |

Quand part le dernier train?
When does the last train go?

J'avais une voiture quand j'habitais à Paris.
I had a car when I lived in Paris.

Viens quand tu auras fini.
Come when you have finished.

L'homme donne un coup de sifflet.
The man is blowing a whistle.

Heidi est la femme de Fritz.
Heidi is Fritz's wife.

| to win | gagner | wing | l'aile (f) | without | sans |

Sam gagne la course.
Sam wins the race.

L'oiseau bat des ailes. *
The bird flaps its wings.

La sorcière est sans son chat.
The witch without her cat.

---

wind — **le vent**

Le vent souffle.
The wind is blowing.

to wipe — **essuyer**

Bill essuie la table.
Bill is wiping the table.

wood — **le bois**

La table est en bois.
The table is made of wood.

---

window — **la vitre**[1]

Le voleur casse la vitre.
The thief breaks the window.

wire — **le fil de fer**

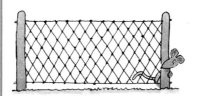

La clôture est en fil de fer.
The fence is made of wire.

wool — **la laine**

Trois pelotes de laine.
Three balls of wool.

---

windmill — **le moulin à vent**

Voici un moulin à vent.
This is a windmill.

witch — **la sorcière**

La sorcière vole.
The witch is flying.

woman — **la femme**

Fifi est une femme.
Fifi is a woman.

---

wine — **le vin**

Henri verse un verre de vin.
Henry pours a glass of wine.

with — **avec**

La sorcière est avec son chat.
The witch is with her cat.

word — **le mot**

Mimi écrit un mot.
Mimi is writing a word.

---

1. **La vitre** is the word for the window pane. The word for window is la fenêtre.

| to **work** | **travailler** | **wrong** | **faux, fausse** | yesterday | **hier** |

Ben travaille dur.
Ben is working hard.

La solution est fausse.
The answer is wrong.

Hier est le jour qui a précédé aujourd'hui. Aujourd'hui c'est lundi, hier c'était dimanche.
Yesterday was the day before today. Today is Monday, yesterday was Sunday.

world   **le monde**

Voici une carte du monde.
This is a map of the world.

young   **jeune**

Un chiot est un jeune chien.
A puppy is a young dog.

worm   **le ver de terre**

L'oiseau regarde le ver de terre.
The bird looks at the worm.

yacht   **le yacht**

Le yacht est en mer.
The yacht is at sea.

to **wrap**   **emballer**

Fifi emballe un cadeau.
Fifi is wrapping a present.

year   **l'année (f)**

Il y a 365 jours dans l'année.
There are 365 days in a year.

Il y a 12 mois ou 52 semaines dans l'année.
There are 12 months or 52 weeks in a year.

zebra   **le zèbre**

Un zèbre a un pelage rayé.
A zebra has a striped coat.

to **write**   **écrire**

Fifi écrit une lettre.
Fifi is writing a letter.

yellow   **jaune**

Le poussin est jaune.
The chick is yellow.

zoo   **le zoo**

Mimi regarde un zèbre au zoo.
Mimi sees a zebra at the zoo.

Pronunciation Guide

In French many letters are pronounced differently from in English. The best way to learn to speak French is to listen carefully to French people and copy what they say, but here are some general points to help you.

Below is a list of letters, with a guide to how to pronounce each one. For each French sound we have shown an English word, or part of a word, which sounds like it. Read it out loud in a normal way to find out how to pronounce the French sound, then practise saying the examples shown beneath.

a   Often like the "a" sound in "cat":
arriver, Paris, chat, mari

e   Like the "a" sound in "above":
le, petit, regarder

é   Like the "ay" sound in "late":
été, café, thé

è   Like the "a" sound in "care":
mère, père

ê   Like the "e" sound in "get":
même, vous êtes

i   Like the "i" in "machine":
il, dix, police, ville

o   Like the "o" in "holiday":
fromage, pomme

u   Round you lips as if to say "oo", then try to say "ee":
du, une, plus, musique

eau, au   Like the "oa" sound in "toast":
eau, beau, gauche, château

eu   Like the "u" sound in "fur":
deux, bleu, cheveu

ou   Like the "oo" sound in "food":
ou, tout, beacoup

oi   Like the "wa" sound in "whack":
voix, poisson, boîte

on, an,   Like "ong" without the "g" sound at the end:
dans, bonjour, français, Avignon

un   Like the "u" sound in "sun". You do not pronounce the "n":
un, chacun

in, ain   Like the "an" sound in "rang" without the "g" at the end:
vin, prince, impossible, train

c   Before "i" or "e" it sounds like the "s" in "sun":
merci, France, certain

Before other letters it sounds like the "c" in "cat":
café, cotton, crabe

ç   Like the "s" in "sun":
garçon, français

ch   Like the "sh" sound in "shirt":
cochon, vache, chanter, Charles

g   Before "i" or "e" it sounds like the "s" sound in "measure":
gendarme, girafe, âge

Before other letters it is like the "g" in "get":
grand, gare, guitare

gn   Like the "ni" sound in "onion":
campagne, montagne

j   Like the soft "g" in girafe above:
bonjour, jeune

th   Like the "t" in "top":
thé, théâtre

qu   Like the "k" sound in "kettle":
question, musique

h   This is not pronounced:
histoire, hôpital, hôtel

A consonant at the end of a French word is not usually pronounced: français, petit, les, tout.

Basic Grammar

French grammar is different from English grammar. These simple notes on basic grammar will help you to understand some of the things you come across in the French sentences in the book.

the

In French every noun is masculine or feminine. The word you use for "the" shows whether the noun is masculine or feminine and also whether it is singular or plural. The word for "the" is **le** before masculine nouns, **la** before feminine nouns and **l'** before nouns beginning with a vowel.

e.g. **le livre**   the book
      la maison   the house
      l'arbre   the tree

The word for "the" is **les** before all plural nouns:

e.g. **les livres**   the books
      les maisons   the houses
      les arbres   the trees

If **le** comes after **à** (to, at) it becomes **au**:
e.g. **Fifi va au cinéma**
      Fifi goes to the cinema

les after **à** becomes **aux**:

e.g. **Ben donne les os aux chiens.**
      Ben gives the bones to the dogs.

If **le** comes after **de** (of), it becomes **du**:

e.g. **le chien du boulanger**
      the dog of the baker

les after **de** becomes **des**:

e.g. **la mère des enfants**
      the mother of the children

a, an

The French for a or an is **un** before masculine nouns and **une** before feminine nouns:

e.g. **un libre**   a book
      une maison   a house
      un arbre   a tree

some, any

The French for "some" or "any" is **du** before a masculine noun, **de la** before a feminine noun, **de l'** before a noun beginning with a vowel and **des** before plural nouns.

e.g. **du lait**   some milk
      de la bière   some beer
      de l'eau   some water
      des pommes   some apples

Pronouns

The French word for "it" or "they" depends on whether the noun it replaces is masculine or feminine.

e.g. **le chat dort**   **il dort**
      the cat sleeps   it sleeps

      la vache dort   **elle dort**
      the cow sleeps   it sleeps

I	**je**	we	**nous**
you	**tu**	you (p)	**vous**
he/it (m)	**il**	they (m)	**ils**
she/it (f)	**elle**	they (f)	**elles**

Possessive pronouns

The word you use for "my", "your", "his", etc., depends on whether the word that follows it is masculine, feminine or plural.

e.g. **mon livre**   my book
      ma maison   my house
      mes frères   my brothers

	(m)	(f)	(pl)
my	mon	ma	mes
your	ton	ta	tes
his/her/its	son	sa	ses
our	notre	notre	nos
your (p)	votre	votre	vos
their	leur	leur	leurs

Adjectives

French adjectives are masculine or feminine to go with the nouns they are describing. You usually add "e" to a masculine singular adjective to make it feminine, unless the adjective already ends in "e".

e.g.
le petit chien	the little dog
la petite chaise	the little chair
le livre vert	the green book
la robe verte	the green dress

You usually add "s" to an adjective to make it plural.

e.g.
les petits chiens	the little dogs
les petites chaises	the little chairs
les livres verts	the green books
les robes vertes	the green dresses

Most French adjectives follow the noun, but some common ones, such as **petit** (little), **bon** (good) and **jeune** (young), come before the noun.

Verbs

The ending of a French verb changes depending on the subject. There are three main types of verb: those ending in **er**, those ending in **ir** and those ending in **re**. Most French verbs follow the pattern of one of these types of verb.

parler	to speak
je parle	I speak
tu parles	you speak
il/elle parle	he/she/it speaks
nous parlons	we speak
vous parlez	you speak (pl)
ils/elles parlent	they speak

finir	to finish
je finis	I finish
tu finis	you finish
il/elle finit	he/she/it finishes
nous finissons	we finish
vous finissez	you finish (pl)
ils/elles finissent	they finish

vendre	to sell
je vends	I sell
tu vends	you sell
il-elle vend	he/she/it sells
nous vendons	we sell
vous vendez	you sell (pl)
ils/elles vendent	they sell

Here are some useful verbs that do not follow any of these patterns.

être	to be
je suis	I am
tu es	you are
il/elle est	he/she/it is
nous sommes	we are
vous êtes	you are (pl)
ils/elles sont	they are

avoir	to have
j'ai	I have
tu as	you have
il/elle a	he/she/it has
nous avons	we have
vous avez	you have (pl)
ils/elles ont	they have

aller	to go
je vais	I go
tu vas	you go
il/elle va	he/she/it goes
nous allons	we go
vous allez	you go (pl)
ils/elles vont	they go

Reflexive verbs

These are verbs which always have a special pronoun in front of them. Where in English we say "I get up" the French say "I get myself up" **Je me lève**. The pronoun changes depending on the subject of the verb:

se lever	to get up
je me lève	I get up
tu te lèves	you get up
il/elle se lève	he/she/it gets up
nous nous levons	we get up
vous vous levez	you get up (pl)
ils/elles se lèvent	they get up

Useful Words and Phrases

Months, Seasons and Days

The French names for the days of the week, the months and the seasons are all masculine. None of them are written with a capital letter at the beginning.

The months

January	janvier
February	février
March	mars
April	avril
May	mai
June	juin
July	juillet
August	août
September	septembre
October	octobre
November	novembre
December	décembre

The seasons

Spring	le printemps
Summer	l'été
Autumn	l'automne
Winter	l'hiver

The days

Monday	lundi
Tuesday	mardi
Wednesday	mercredi
Thursday	jeudi
Friday	vendredi
Saturday	samedi
Sunday	dimanche

Numbers and Telling the Time

1	un	13	treize	32	trente-deux	80	quatre-vingts
2	deux	14	quatorze	40	quarante	81	quatre-vingt-un
3	trois	15	quinze	50	cinquante	90	quatre-vingt-dix
4	quatre	16	seize	60	soixante	91	quatre-vingt-onze
5	cinq	17	dix-sept	70	soixante-dix	92	quatre-vingt-douze
6	six	18	dix-huit	71	soixante-onze	100	cent
7	sept	19	dix-neuf	72	soixante-douze	101	cent un
8	huit	20	vingt	73	soixante-treize	150	cent cinquante
9	neuf	21	vingt et un	74	soixante-quatorze	200	deux cents
10	dix	22	vingt-deux	75	soixante-quinze	201	deux cent un
11	onze	30	trente	76	soixante-seize	500	cinq cents
12	douze	31	trente et un	77	soixante-dix-sept	1000	mille

Telling the time

What is the time?	Quelle heure est-il?
It is nine o'clock	Il est neuf heures
It is five past nine	Il est neuf heures cinq
It is a quarter past nine	Il est neuf heures et quart
It is half past nine	Il est neuf heures et demie
It is a quarter to ten	Il est dix heures moins le quart
It is five to ten	Il est dix heures moins cinq
It is midday/midnight	Il est midi/minuit

Countries and Continents

Africa	l'Afrique (f)	India	l'Inde (f)
Asia	l'Asie (f)	Ireland	l'Irlande (f)
Australia	l'Australie (f)	Italy	l'Italie (f)
Austria	l'Autriche (f)	Japan	le Japon
Belgium	la Belgique	The Netherlands	les Pays Bas (m)
Canada	le Canada	New Zealand	la Nouvelle-Zélande
China	la Chine	Poland	la Pologne
Czechoslovakia	la Tchécoslovaquie	Scotland	l'Ecosse (f)
Denmark	le Danemark	South America	l'Amérique du Sud
England	l'Angleterre (f)	Soviet Union	l'Union soviétique (f)
Europe	l'Europe (f)	Spain	l'Espagne (f)
France	la France	Switzerland	la Suisse
Germany	l'Allemagne (f)	United States	les Etats-Unis (m)
Great Britain	la Grande Bretagne	Wales	le pays de Galles
Hungary	la Hongroie	Yugoslavia	la Yougoslavie

Useful Words and Phrases

Yes	Oui
No	Non
Please	S'il vous plaît
I would like . . .	Je voudrais . . .
Thank you	Merci
I'm sorry	Pardon
Excuse me	Excusez-moi
Mr	Monsieur
Mrs	Madame
Miss	Mademoiselle
I do not understand.	Je ne comprends pas.
I do not speak French.	Je ne parle pas français.
Please speak more slowly.	Plus lentement, s'il vous plaît.

Making friends

Hello	Bonjour
Good evening	Bonsoir
Good night	Bonne nuit
Goodbye	Au revoir
What is your name?	Comment t'appelles-tu?
My name is Roger.	Je m'appelle Roger.
How are you?	Comment vas-tu?
I am well, thank you.	Je vais bien, merci.

Asking the way

Where is . . . ?	Où est . . . ?
Where are . . . ?	Où sont . . . ?
How do I get to the station please?	Pour aller à la gare s'il vous plaît?
You go . . .	Vous allez . . .
You carry on . . .	Vous continuez . . .
You turn . . .	Vous tournez
to the right	à droite
to the left	à gauche
straight ahead	tout droit

Useful places to ask for

airport	l'aéroport
bank	la banque
campsite	le camping
chemist	la pharmacie
hospital	l'hôpital
police station	la gendarmerie
post office	le bureau de poste
station	la gare
tourist office	le syndicat d'initiative
youth hostel	l'auberge de jeunesse

Index

le blé	corn	20
bleu	blue	10
blond	fair	28
le blue-jean	jeans	39
le bocal	jar	39
le boeuf	beef	9
boire	to drink	25
le bois	wood	79
la boîte	box	11
bon marché	cheap	16
bon, bonne	good	33
bon, bonne	kind	40
le bonbon	sweet	69
le bord	bank	8
le bord	edge	26
la bosse	bump	13
la botte	boot	11
la bouche	mouth	47
le boucher	butcher	14
le bouchon	cork	20
la boue	mud	47
la bougie	candle	15
la bouilloire	kettle	39
le boulanger	baker	7
le bouquet	bunch	13
le bourgeon	bud	12
le bout	end	26
la bouteille	bottle	11
le bouton	button	14
le bouton	spot	66
le bracelet	bracelet	11
la branche	branch	11
le bras	arm	6
brillant	bright	12
la brique	brick	12
la brosse à cheveux	hairbrush	34
la brosse à dents	toothbrush	73
brosser	to brush	12
la brouette	wheelbarrow	78
le brouillard	fog	30
le bruit	noise	48
brûler	to burn	13
brun	brown	12
brusquement	suddenly	68
bruyant	loud	44
le buisson	bush	13
le bulbe	bulb	13
le bulldozer	bulldozer	13
la bulle	bubble	12
le bureau	desk	23
le bureau	office	49
la cabane	hut	37
se cacher	hide	36
le cadeau	present	55
le café	café	14
le café	coffee	19
la cage	cage	14
le cahier	exercise book	27
la calculatrice	calculator	14
le calendrier	calendar	14
le cambrioleur	burglar	13
le camion	lorry	44
la camionette	van	75
la campagne	country	20

camper	to camp	15
le canapé	sofa	65
le canard	duck	25
la capitale	capital	15
le car	coach	19
la caravane	caravan	15
le cardigan	cardigan	15
le carnet	notebook	49
la carotte	carrot	15
le carré	square	66
le carrefour	crossroads	21
le cartable	satchel	60
la carte	card	15
la carte	map	45
la carte postale	postcard	55
la casquette	cap	15
casser	to break	12
la casserole	saucepan	60
la cave	cellar	
ce, cette, cet	that	61
ce, cette, cet	this	72
la ceinture	belt	9
célèbre	famous	28
le cercle	circle	18
le cerf	deer	23
le cerf-volant	kite	40
la cerise	cherry	17
certain	some	65
la chaîne	chain	16
la chaîne stéréo	stereo	67
la chaise	chair	16
la chambre	bedroom	9
le chameau	camel	14
le champ	field	29
le champignon	mushroom	47
changer	to change	16
la chanson	song	66
chanter	to sing	63
le chapeau	hat	35
chaque	each	25
le chat	cat	15
le château	castle	15
le chaton	kitten	40
chaud	warm	77
chaud	hot	37
la chaussette	sock	65
la chaussure	shoe	63
le chef d'orchestre	conductor	20
le chemin	path	52
la cheminée	chimney	17
la chemise	shirt	63
la chenille	caterpillar	16
le chèque	cheque	17
chercher	to look for	44
le cheval	horse	37
les cheveux (m. pl)	hair	34
la chèvre	goat	33
le chien	dog	24
le chimpanzé	chimpanzee	17
le chiot	puppy	56
le chocolat	chocolate	17
choisir	to choose	17
la chose	thing	71
le chou	cabbage	14
le chou-fleur	cauliflower	16

chuchoter	to whisper	78	la couverture	blanket	10
la chute d'eau	waterfall	77	couvrir	to cover	20
le ciel	sky	64	le cowboy	cowboy	21
la cigarette	cigarette	18	le crabe	crab	21
le cinéma	cinema	18	la craie	chalk	16
cirer	to polish	54	la cravate	tie	72
le cirque	circus	18	le crayon	pencil	52
les ciseaux (m)	scissors	61	le crayon de couleur	crayon	21
le citron	lemon	42	la crème	cream	21
la classe	class	18	la crêpe	pancake	51
la classe	classroom	18	creuser	to dig	23
la clé	key	39	crier	to shout	63
le client	customer	22	le crochet	hook	37
la cloche	bell	9	le crocodile	crocodile	21
la clôture	fence	29	croire	to believe	9
le clou	nail	47	la croix	cross	21
le clown	clown	19	la cruche	jug	39
le cochon	pig	53	le cube	cube	21
le coeur	heart	35	cueillir	to pick	53
le coiffeur	hairdresser	34	la cuiller	spoon	66
le coin	corner	20	le cuir	leather	42
le collant	tights	72	la cuisine	kitchen	40
le collier	necklace	48	la cuisinière	cooker	20
la colline	hill	26	le cygne	swan	69
commander	to order	50			
comme	as	7	le danger	danger	22
commencer	to begin	9	dans	in	38
commencer	to start	67	danser	to dance	22
comment	how	37	la danseuse	dancer	22
comprendre	to understand	75	de	from	31
compter	to count	20	déchirer	to tear	70
le concombre	cucumber	21	décider	to decide	22
conduire	to drive	25	découper	to cut out	22
la confiture	jam	39	décrire	to describe	23
congeler	to freeze	31	dehors	outside	50
connaître	to know	41	déjà	already	5
construire	to build	13	déjeuner	to have lunch	44
content	happy	35	demain	tomorrow	73
contre	against	4	demander	to ask (for)	7
le coq	cockerel	19	la dentelle	lace	41
le coquillage	shell	62	le dentifrice	toothpaste	73
la corde	rope	59	le dentiste	dentist	23
le corps	body	11	les dents (m)	teeth	70
le costume	suit	69	se dépêcher	to hurry	37
la côte	coast	19	dépenser	to spend	66
le côté	side	63	déplacer	to move	47
la côtelette	chop	17	depuis	since	63
le coton	cotton	20	dernier	last	41
le cou	neck	48	derrière	behind	9
le coude	elbow	26	des	any	6
coudre	to sew	62	le désert	desert	23
la couette	duvet	25	déshabiller	to undress	75
couler	to flow	30	le dessert	pudding	56
la couleur	colour	19	le dessin	drawing	24
les couleurs (pl)	paints	51	dessiner	to draw	24
la coupe	bowl	11	les deux	both	11
couper	to cut	22	devant	in front of	31
courir	to run	59	les devoirs (m)	homework	37
la couronne	crown	21	le diamant	diamond	23
la course	race	57	la diapositive	slide	64
court	short	63	le dictionnaire	dictionary	23
le coussin	cushion	22	différent	different	23
le couteau	knife	40	le dîner	dinner	23
coûter	to cost	20	le dinosaure	dinosaur	23
la couvercle	lid	42	dire	to say	61

la direction	direction	23
se disputer	to argue	6
le disque	record	58
le doigt	finger	29
le doigt de pied	toe	72
donner	to give	33
donner un coup de pied	to kick	40
dormir	to sleep	64
le dos	back	7
la douche	shower	63
le dragon	dragon	24
le drap	sheet	62
le drapeau	flag	30
droit	straight	68
droite	right	58
drôle	funny	32
dur	hard	35
durer	to last	41
l'eau(f)	water	447
l'écharpe (f)	scarf	61
l'échelle (f)	ladder	41
l'éclair (m)	lightning	43
l'école (f)	school	61
écouter	to listen	43
écrire	to write	80
l'écriteau (m)	notice	49
l'écurie (f)	stable	67
égaré	lost	44
l'église (f)	church	18
l'éléphant (m)	elephant	26
emballer	to wrap	80
embrasser	to kiss	40
en	of	49
en bas	downstairs	24
en colère	angry	5
en face de	opposite	50
en haut	upstairs	75
en retard	late	41
encore	again	4
l'endroit (m)	place	54
les enfants (m)	children	17
ensemble	together	72
entendre	to hear	35
entourer	to surround	69
entre	between	10
l'entrée (f)	entrance	26
entrer	to enter	26
l'enveloppe (f)	envelope	26
envoyer	to send	62
épais, épaisse	thick	71
l'épaule (f)	shoulder	63
épeler	to spell	66
l'épicier (m)	grocer	33
l'épingle (f)	pin	53
épouser	to marry	45
l'équipe (f)	team	70
escalader	to climb	18
l'escalier (m)	stairs	67
l'escargot (m)	snail	65
l'espace (m)	space	66
l'essence (f)	petrol	52
essuyer	to wipe	79
l'est (m)	east	26
et	and	5

étaler	to spread	66
l'étoile (f)	star	67
être assis	to sit	63
s'évader	to escape	26
l'expérience (f)	experiment	27
expliquer	to explain	27
facile	easy	26
le facteur	postman	55
faible	weak	77
faire	to do	24
faire	to make	44
faire cuire	to fry	31
faire la cuisine	to cook	20
faire du ski	to ski	64
faire du voilier	to sail	60
faire peur (à)	to frighten	31
faire semblant (de)	to pretend	55
faire un noeud	to tie a knot	72
la falaise	cliff	18
la famille	family	28
la fanfare	band	8
le fantôme	ghost	32
la farine	flour	30
fatigué	tired	72
le fauteuil	armchair	6
faux, fausse	wrong	80
la fée	fairy	28
la femme	wife	78
la femme	woman	79
la fenêtre	window	79
le fer à repasser	iron	38
la ferme	farm	28
fermé	shut	63
fermer	to close	18
le fermier	farmer	28
la fête	party	51
le feu	fire	29
le feu de joie	bonfire	11
la feuille	leaf	42
les feux	traffic lights	73
les feux d'artifice (m)	fireworks	29
la ficelle	string	68
la figure	face	27
le fil de fer	wire	79
la fille	daughter	22
la fille	girl	32
le film	film	29
le fils	son	65
finir	to finish	29
la flamme	flame	30
la flèche	arrow	6
la fleur	flower	30
le foin	hay	35
fondre	to melt	45
la forêt	forest	31
la forme	shape	62
fort	strong	68
la fourchette	fork	31
la fourmi	ant	6
la fourrure	fur	32
la fraise	strawberry	68
la framboise	raspberry	57
frapper	to hit	36
frapper	to knock	40

le frère	brother	12
les frites (f)	chips	17
froid	cold	19
le fromage	cheese	16
le front	forehead	31
se frotter	to rub	59
le fruit	fruit	31
fumer	to smoke	65
gagner	to win	79
le gant	glove	33
le garage	garage	32
le garçon	boy	11
le garçon	waiter	76
garder	to keep	39
la gare	station	67
garer	to park	51
le gâteau	cake	14
gauche	left	42
le gaz	gas	32
le gazon	lawn	41
le géant	giant	32
le gel	frost	31
geler	to freeze	31
le gendarme	policeman	54
le genou	knee	40
les gens (m)	people	52
la girafe	giraffe	32
la glace	ice	38
la glace	ice cream	38
la glace	mirror	46
glisser	to slide	64
goûter	to taste	70
la graine	seed	61
grand	tall	70
grandir	to grow	34
se gratter	to scratch	61
la grenouille	frog	31
gris	grey	33
gros, grosse	big	10
gros, grosse	fat	28
le groupe	group	34
la grue	crane	21
la guêpe	wasp	77
la guerre	war	77
la guitare	guitar	34
habiller	to dress	24
la haie	hedge	36
le haricot	bean	8
le haut	top	73
haut	high	36
l'hélicoptère (m)	helicopter	36
l'herbe (f)	grass	33
le hérisson	hedgehog	36
l'heure (f)	hour	37
le hibou	owl	50
hier	yesterday	80
l'hippopotame (m)	hippopotamus	36
l'histoire (f)	story	68
l'homme (m)	man	45
l'hôpital (m)	hospital	37
l'horloge (f)	clock	18
hors de	out of	50
l'hôtel (m)	hotel	37

huiler	to oil	49
ici	here	36
l'idée (f)	idea	38
l'île (f)	island	38
l'illustré (m)	comic	19
l'imperméable (m)	raincoat	57
important	important	38
l'infirmière (f)	nurse	49
l'insecte (m)	insect	38
intelligent	clever	18
l'invité	guest	34
inviter	to invite	38
la jambe	leg	42
le jambon	ham	34
le jardin	garden	32
jaune	yellow	80
jeter	to throw	72
le jeu	game	32
jeune	young	80
joli	pretty	55
la joue	cheek	16
jouer	to play	54
le jouet	toy	73
le jour	day	22
le journal	newspaper	48
le jumeau, la jumelle	twin	74
la jupe	skirt	64
jusqu'à	until	75
le kangourou	kangaroo	39
là	there	71
le lac	lake	41
laid	ugly	74
la laine	wool	79
la laisse	lead	41
laisser tomber	to drop	25
le lait	milk	46
la laitue	lettuce	42
la lampe	lamp	41
le landau	pram	55
la langue	tongue	73
le lapin	rabbit	57
large	wide	78
la larme	tear	70
le lavabo	wash basin	77
se laver	to wash	77
le long de	along	5
lécher	to lick	42
la leçon	lesson	42
léger	light	43
le légume	vegetable	76
lentement	slowly	64
la lettre	letter	42
se lever	to get up	32
la lèvre	lip	43
la librairie	bookshop	11
le lion	lion	43
lire	to read	57
la liste	list	43
le lit	bed	8
le livre	book	11
loin	far	28

long, longue	long	44		monter à	to ride	58
lorsque	as	7		la montre	watch	77
lourd	heavy	35		montrer	to show	63
la lumière	light	43		montrer du doigt	to point	54
la lune	moon	46		le morceau	piece	53
les lunettes (f. pl)	glasses	33		mordre	to bite	10
				mort	dead	22
la machine	machine	44		le mot	word	79
la machine à coudre	sewing machine	62		la moto	motorbike	47
la machine à écrire	typewriter	74		la mouche	fly	30
la machine à laver	washing machine	77		le mouchoir	handkerchief	35
le magasin	shop	63		mouillé	wet	78
maigre	thin	61		le moulin à vent	windmill	79
le maillot de bain	swimsuit	69		mourir	to die	23
la main	hand	34		la moustache	moustache	47
maintenant	now	49		le mouton	sheep	62
mais	but	13		le mur	wall	76
la maison	house	37		la musique	music	47
malade	ill	38				
le malade	patient	52		nager	to swim	69
la manche	sleeve	64		le navire	ship	62
manger	to eat	26		ne . . . jamais	never	48
le manteau	coat	19		neiger	to snow	65
le marché	market	45		nettoyer	to clean	18
la marche	step	67		le nez	nose	48
la mare	pond	54		la niche	kennel	39
le mari	husband	37		le nid	nest	48
le mariage	wedding	77		Noël	Christmas	17
le marié	bridegroom	12		le noeud	knot	40
la mariée	bride	12		noir	black	10
le marin	sailor	60		la noix	nut	49
la marionnette	puppet	56		le nom	name	47
le marteau	hammer	34		le nombre	number	49
le masque	mask	45		le nord	north	48
le matin	morning	46		nourrir	to feed	28
mauvais	bad	7		la nourriture	food	30
mauvais	rough	59		nouveau, nouvelle	new	48
mécontent	unhappy	75		le nuage	cloud	19
le médecin	doctor	24		la nuit	night	48
le médicament	medicine	45				
le meilleur, la meilleure	best	9		occupé	busy	13
même	same	60		l'oeil, les yeux (m)	eye, eyes	27
mener	to lead	41		l'oeuf (m)	egg	26
le menton	chin	17		offrir	to offer	49
le menu	menu	45		l'oie (f)	goose	33
la mer	sea	61		l'oignon (m)	onion	50
la mère	mother	47		l'oiseau (m)	bird	10
le merle	blackbird	10		l'ombre (f)	shadow	62
mesurer	to measure	45		l'oncle (m)	uncle	75
le métal	metal	46		l'or (m)	gold	33
le métro	underground	75		l'orage (m)	storm	68
mettre	to put	56		orange	orange	50
le miel	honey	37		l'orange (f)	orange	50
mieux	better	10		l'ordinateur (m)	computer	20
le milieu	middle	46		l'oreille (f)	ear	25
la minute	minute	46		l'oreiller (m)	pillow	53
le modèle réduit	model	46		l'os (m)	bone	11
moelleux, moelleuse	soft	65		oser	to dare	22
le mois	month	46		ou	or	50
la moitié	half	34		où	where	78
le monde	world	80		oublier	to forget	31
la monnaie	change	16		l'ouest (m)	west	78
le monstre	monster	46		l'ours (m)	bear	8
la montagne	mountain	47		l'ours en peluche (m)	teddy bear	70
monter	to go up	75		l'outil (m)	tool	73

ouvert	open	50		la pierre	stone	67
ouvrir	to open	50		la pieuvre	octopus	49
				la pile	pile	53
la page	page	51		le pilote	pilot	53
le pain	bread	12		pincer	to pinch	53
la paire	pair	51		la pipe	pipe	54
le palais	palace	51		le pique-nique	picnic	53
le pamplemousse	grapefruit	33		la piscine	swimming pool	69
le panier	basket	8		le pistolet	gun	34
le pantalon	trousers	74		le placard	cupboard	21
la pantoufle	slipper	64		la plafond	ceiling	16
le papier	paper	51		la plage	beach	8
le papier peint	wallpaper	76		la plaisanterie	joke	39
le papillon	butterfly	14		le plancher	floor	30
Pâques	Easter	26		la plante	plant	54
le paquet	parcel	51		planter	to plant	54
par	through	72		le plat	dish	25
par-dessus	over	50		plat	flat	30
le parachute	parachute	51		plein	full	31
le parapluie	umbrella	74		pleurer	to cry	21
le parc	park	51		pleuvoir	to rain	57
parce que	because	8		plier	to bend	9
les parents (m)	parents	51		la plume	feather	28
paresseux, euse	lazy	41		la plupart	most	46
parler	to speak	66		plus	more	46
parmi	among	5		le pneu	tyre	74
partager	to share	62		la poche	pocket	54
partout	everywhere	27		la poêle	frying pan	32
le passeport	passport	52		la poire	pear	52
se passer	to happen	35		le poireau	leek	42
passer devant	to pass	51		le poisson	fish	29
passionnant	exciting	27		la poitrine	chest	17
patiner	to skate	63		le poivre	pepper	52
la patte	paw	52		poli	polite	54
pauvre	poor	54		la pomme	apple	6
payer	to pay	52		la pomme de terre	potato	55
le pays	country	20		le pompier	fireman	29
la peau	skin	64		le poney	pony	54
la pêche	peach	52		le pont	bridge	12
pêcher à la ligne	to fish	29		le porc	pork	55
le peigne	comb	19		le port	harbour	35
se peigner	to comb	19		le port	port	55
peindre	to paint	51		la porte	door	24
la pelle	spade	66		le porte-monnaie	purse	56
pendant	while	78		porter	to wear	77
penser	to think	71		porter	to carry	15
le père	father	28		le porteur	porter	55
le perroquet	parrot	51		la poste	post office	55
personne	nobody	48		la poubelle	dustbin	25
peser	to weigh	77		le pouce	thumb	72
le petit déjeuner	breakfast	12		la poule	hen	36
petit	small	65		le poulet	chicken	17
les petits pois (m)	peas	52		la poupée	doll	24
peu	few	29		pour	for	30
peut-être	perhaps	52		pourpre	purple	56
la phare	lighthouse	43		pourquoi	why	78
les phares (f)	headlights	35		poursuivre	to chase	16
le pharmacien	chemist	17		pousser	to push	56
le phoque	seal	61		la poussière	dust	25
le photo	photograph	53		le poussin	chick	17
la phrase	sentence	62		premier, ière	first	29
le piano	piano	53		prendre	to make	70
la pièce	coin	19		près (de)	near	48
la pièce	room	59		presque	almost	5
les pieds (m)	feet	28		le prestidigitateur	magician	44

le prix	price	55	le riz	rice	58
le prix	prize	55	la robe	dress	24
le professeur	teacher	70	le robinet	tap	70
profond	deep	23	le rocher	rock	59
la promenade	walk	76	le roi	king	40
promettre	to promise	55	rond	round	59
propre	clean	18	rose	pink	54
puis	then	71	la rose	rose	59
puisque	since	63	la roue	wheel	78
le puzzle	puzzle	56	rouge	red	58
le pyjama	pyjamas	56	la route	road	59
			le ruban	ribbon	58
quand	when	78	la rue	street	68
quel, quelle	which	78	rugir	to roar	59
quelqu'un	anybody	6	le ruisseau	stream	68
quelqu'un	someone	65			
quelque chose	something	65	le sable	sand	60
quelquefois	sometimes	65	le sac	bag	7
la question	question	56	le sac	sack	60
la queue	queue	56	le sac à main	handbag	34
la queue	tail	70	sain et sauf	safe	60
qui	who	78	la salade	salad	60
quitter	to leave	42	sale	dirty	24
			la salle à manger	dining room	23
la racine	root	59	la salle de bains	bathroom	8
raconter	to tell	71	le salon	sitting room	63
le radiateur	radiator	57	la sandale	sandal	60
la radio	radio	57	le sandwich	sandwich	60
le raisin	grape	33	le sang	blood	10
ramasser	to pick up	53	sans	without	79
ramer	to row	59	la sauce	sauce	60
le rang	row	59	la saucisse	sausage	61
la rangée	line	43	sauf	except	27
se rappeler de	to remember	58	sauter	to jump	39
le rasoir	razor	57	savoir	to know	41
le rat	rat	57	le savon	soap	65
rater	to miss	46	la scie	saw	61
rayé	striped	68	le seau	bucket	12
recevoir	to receive	58	sec, sèche	dry	25
reconnaître	to recognise	58	secouer	to shake	62
le réfrigérateur	fridge	31	le sel	salt	60
refuser	to refuse	58	sembler	to seem	61
regarder	to look at	44	sentir	to smell	65
la reine	queen	56	le serpent	snake	65
remercier	to thank	71	la serviette	towel	73
remplir	to fill	29	servir	to serve	62
le renard	fox	31	se servir de	to use	75
rencontrer	to meet	45	seul	alone	5
rendre visite à	to visit	76	seulement	only	50
réparer	to mend	45	le short	shorts	63
repasser	to iron	38	le sifflet	whistle	78
la réponse	answer	4	silencieusement	quietly	56
se reposer	to rest	58	le singe	monkey	46
le requin	shark	62	les skis (m)	skis	64
respirer	to breathe	12	la soeur	sister	63
rester	to stay	67	le soir	evening	26
le réveil	alarm clock	5	le sol	ground	34
se réveiller	to wake up	76	le soldat	soldier	65
rêver	to dream	24	le soleil	sun	69
la revue	magazine	44	la solution	answer	4
riche	rich	58	sombre	dark	22
le rideau	curtain	22	sonner	to ring	58
rien	nothing	49	la sorcière	witch	79
rire	to laugh	41	la sorte	kind	40
la rivière	river	59	la sorte	sort	66

la soucoupe	saucer	61	le tracteur	tractor	73
souffler	to blow	10	le train	train	74
soulever	to lift	43	la tranche	slice	64
la soupe	soup	66	travailler	to work	80
sourire	to smile	65	traverser	to cross	21
la souris	mouse	47	très	very	76
sous	under	75	le trésor	treasure	74
le sous-marin	submarine	68	le triangle	triangle	74
se souvenir (de)	to remember	58	le tricot	knitting	40
souvent	often	49	tricoter	to knit	40
la statue	statue	67	triste	sad	60
le stylo	pen	52	la trompette	trumpet	74
le sucre	sugar	68	trop	too	73
le sud	south	66	le trottoir	pavement	52
suivre	to follow	30	le trou	hole	36
le supermarché	supermarket	69	trouver	to find	29
sur	about	4	tuer	to kill	40
sur	on	49			
la surprise	surprise	69	l'usine (f)	factory	27
suspendre	to hang	35	utile	useful	75
la table	table	69	les vacances (f)	holiday	36
le tableau	picture	53	la vache	cow	20
le tableau noir	blackboard	10	la vague	wave	77
le tablier	apron	6	la valise	suitcase	68
la tache	mark	45	la vallée	valley	75
le tambour	drum	25	le vase	vase	76
la tante	aunt	7	le veau	calf	14
taper à la machine	to type	74	vendre	to sell	61
le tapis	carpet	15	venir	to come	19
tard	late	41	le vent	wind	79
la tarte	pie	53	le ver de terre	worm	80
la tasse	cup	21	le verre	glass	33
le taureau	bull	13	vers	towards	73
le taxi	taxi	70	verser	to pour	55
le téléphone	telephone	70	vert	green	33
la télévision	television	71	la veste	jacket	39
tenir	to hold	36	la viande	meat	45
se tenir debout	to stand	67	vide	empty	26
le tennis	tennis	71	vider	to empty	26
la tente	tent	71	la vie	life	43
la terre	earth	25	vieux, vieille	old	49
la tête	head	35	le village	village	76
le thé	tea	70	vilain	naughty	47
le théâtre	theatre	71	la ville	town	73
la théière	teapot	70	le vin	wine	79
la tige	stem	67	le violin	violin	76
le tigre	tiger	72	vite	fast	28
le timbre	stamp	67	vivre	to live	43
tirer	to pull	56	voici	this is	72
la toile d'araignée	cobweb	19	la voie ferrée	railway line	57
le toit	roof	59	voilà	that is	71
la tomate	tomato	72	voir	to see	61
tomber	to fall	28	la voiture	car	15
tôt	early	25	la voix	voice	76
toucher	to touch	73	voler	to fly	30
toucher	to feel	68	voler	to steal	67
toujours	always	5	le voleur	thief	71
la tour	tower	73	vouloir	to want	76
tourner	to turn	74	vrai	real	58
tous, toutes	all	5			
tous, toutes	every	27	le yacht	yacht	80
tousser	to cough	20			
tout	everything	27	le zèbre	zebra	80
tout le monde	everyone	27	le zoo	zoo	80